Tee Parties

Peg Nikoden

First Edition
Published by MJN Publishing

ISBN 0-9742399-0-9
Library of Congress Control Number: 2003094237

Printed by Minors Printing Company
Boone, North Carolina 28607

Illustrated by Wesley Allsbrook

A percentage of the proceeds from the sale of this book will
be donated to the Avery County Animal Welfare Society,
Avery County, North Carolina.

Tee Parties

An invaluable guide for all aspects of planning golf tournaments.

Themes
Decorations
Invitations
Menus, including recipes
Formats
Prizes

Table of Contents

Acknowledgements

I wish to thank my family and friends for their support and encouragement in this endeavor, especially my husband who patiently endured my many hours at the computer, and my granddaughter, Wesley Allsbrook, a talented young lady who did the illustrations for me. Wesley is presently a student at the Rhode Island School of Design, and has her sights set on a career in illustration.

Thank you also to the PGA of America for allowing the use of their chapter on Formats from the PGA of America Tournament Book.

Thanks to Billy Cleveland and Vicki McClurgh, golf professionals, for their help and endorsements.

Thank you to my son, Paul Nikoden, for creating the website for the book.

Thank you to my daughter Cathy Kirk for her input.

Thank you also to Vikki Cooper at Minors Printing for her patience and hard work in preparing the book for publication. Her attention to detail and prompt response to questions was much appreciated.

This book is dedicated to all the chairpersons and their committees who shoulder the job of running a tournament. I hope the book will be helpful in the ongoing quest for making it the one to be remembered.

Endorsements

As the Director of Golf at Elk River, I have had the opportunity to work alongside the author for several years. Her inquisitive attitude and attention to detail has enabled her to compile "Tee Parties." The examples, tips and recommendations are well thought out and will enhance your effectiveness when asked to serve on a tournament committee. The readers of this book are gaining a wealth of enjoyable information from a true lady who is remarkably dedicated to the game of golf.

Billy Cleveland
Director of Golf
Elk River Club
Banner Elk, NC

"Tee Parties" is a must read for any Tournament Chairperson from novice to experienced. This book is a clear, concise guide to running a club event. Peg Nikoden guides you effortlessly step by step through the entire process from sending invitations to creating delicious meals. She has compiled years of experience in this arena, and has written the only how-to book of its kind. I highly recommend this reading for any Chairperson or Club Official wishing to make their tournament event run as smoothly as possible.

Vicki McClurgh, PGA Member
Former Teaching Professional
Elk River Club, Banner Elk, NC
Presently Head Professional
Cedar Rock Country Club
Lenoir, NC

Ode to a Chairperson

You've been begged, cajoled, and finally inducted.
There is a tournament to be conducted.

Thinking and planning, ideas galore
Let *Tee Parties* help you, that's what it's for.
Decorations, menus, formats and favors,
Invitations, recipes and suggestions
It's a wealth of information, without question.

So delve in this treasure and enjoy all the pages
And have a tournament to remember for ages.

The Ball

In my hand I hold a ball
White and dimpled, rather small
Oh, how bland it does appear
This harmless looking little sphere.

By its size I could not guess
The awesome power it does possess;
But since I fell beneath its spell
I've wandered through the fires of Hell.

My life has not been quite the same
Since I chose to play this game
It rules my mind for hours on end,
A fortune it has made me spend.

It has been my curse and cry.
I hate myself and want to die.
It promises a thing called "par"
If I can hit it straight and far.

To master such a tiny ball
Should not be very hard at all.
But my desires the ball refuses
And does exactly as it chooses.

It hooks and slides…dribbles…Dies
Or disappears before my eyes
Often it will have a whim
To hit a tree or take a swim.

With miles of grass on which to land
It finds a tiny patch of sand.
Then has me offering up my soul
If it will just drop in the hole.

It's made me whimper like a pup
And swear that I will give it up
And take to drink to ease my sorrow…
But "The Ball" knows…
I'll be back…tomorrow.

Beginning to Plan

Beginning to Plan

A good party planner usually starts with an idea, or theme and this plan is carried out throughout the tournament.

This list of suggestions in no way, limits your choices. The possibilities are endless. Have your committee put their heads together and you will be amazed what they come up with. Themes can be based on seasons, holidays, movies, countries, food, flowers, celebrities, animals, birds, music, nursery rhymes, cartoon characters, patriotism, casinos, historic eras, western, outer space, signs of the zodiac, and ad infinitum!

After you have chosen a theme all your party planning can commence. The idea is incorporated into invitations, decorations, menus and prizes. So let the fun begin!

Chart for organizing the tournament

Name of the Event
Day and Date
Type of Event
Size of the field or number of players
Committee Members
Type of Scoring
Special Events—Closest to the Pin
                Longest Drive
                Closest to the Line
Number of prizes to be awarded
                Low Gross
                Low Net
Photographs

Time Schedule
Breakfast, lunch or dinner
Clinic
Putting Contest
Tee times start/Shotgun Start
Prizes Awarded

TOURNAMENT ASSIGNMENT SHEET

TOURNAMENT _____ **DATE** _____

CHAIRMAN_____ **DATE NOTICE CHECKED** _____ **DATE MAILED** _____

NUMBER OF PLAYERS: MEMBERS_____ GUESTS_____

TYPE OF COMPETITION _____

SPECIAL EVENTS: LONG DRIVE HOLE _____

CLOSEST TO HOLE _____

DROP CLUB SIGN _____

PRIZES: _____

VENDOR: _____

NUMBER: _____ **DATE ORDERED:** _____

TOURNAMENT OPERATION:

SCORE CARDS _____ SCORE SHEETS _____

STARTING TEE SETUP _____ SIGN IN TABLE _____

LOUD SPEAKER _____ TYPE OF START _____

PRACTICE FACILITY _____ SETUP TIME _____

GUEST TAGS _____ MEMBER TAGS _____

STARTING TIMES _____ PAIRING _____

ASSIGN CARTS AND CADDIES _____ CLUBS BACK IN CARS_____

MAKE TAGS FOR CARTS _____

RAIN PLAN _____ RULES SHEET _____

HANDICAPS _____ EXTRA CARTS _____

GOLF COURSE PREPARATION:

TEE MARKER LOCATIONS_____ HOLE LOCATIONS _____

GROUND UNDER REPAIR _____ HAZARDS STAKED _____

SPECIAL EVENTS:

FIRST TEE TIME _____ WHERE _____

GREEN CUT _____ FAIRWAY TEES CUT _____

MISC:

Duties of the Professional

Your professional will be your best help in setting up and running the tournament. Rely on his knowledge and experience to assist you. Work together for success.

A well organized plan and good supportive staff will assure you that all aspects of the tournament run smoothly.

The professionals' responsibilities should include:

Announcements

A welcome to the field and instructions for play.

Introduction of the tournament committee and awarding of prizes at the close of the tournament.

Arranging for Hole-in-One insurance if there is to be a large hole-in-one prize.

Golf cart and bag room employee supervision and co-ordination.

Marked scorecards for each golf cart.

Preparation of the putting green if there is to be a putting contest. Assigning staff to create and supervise the putting contest.

Registration Table Preparation
On the first day of a tournament, a table should be set up either at the bag drop, or in close proximity to the pro shop for members and guests to check in. This table should be attractively draped, perhaps decorated with something in relation to the theme of the tournament, or with a bouquet of flowers. Favors may be given at the time of registration along with the schedule and program of events. Tees, ball markers, extra scorecards, pencils, and ball mark repair tools are usually available at this table. The table is manned by the pro shop staff, which shall be appropriately dressed and offer a warm welcome to the participants.

Rules
A rule sheet should be provided for each team. It should include general rules of play and any local or conditional exceptions.
The pro will be the referee in resolving questions regarding rules.

Scoreboard and scoring

Staff Supervision
Instructing the staff how to be the most helpful to players. Setting standards of etiquette and dress code for the staff. (Having the staff dressed alike presents a good image for the club and quickly identifies them for both members and guests.)

The pro will work with the green keeper to provide the best possible conditions for the players. Ground under repair to be plainly marked, as well as hazards, either lateral, marked by red stakes, or water hazards, marked by yellow stakes and out of bounds, marked by white stakes. These hazards are also frequently or additionally, lined with paint.

Prior to the tournament, in the event of rain, ask your professional to prepare a talk on course management as you play, the psychology of match play, rules, or other related topics.

Starters and Rangers
The professional should instruct the starter in a tee time tournament to make certain that groups are teed off in order and precisely on time. Before tee off in the professional's announcements, he should remind players to pick up if they are out of the hole to speed up play. This is most important if the field is full. The ranger should be instructed to keep the field moving if there are any gaps or holes open ahead of the group.

Tee positions
Making certain tee markers are set in the correct location.

SAMPLE HOLE LOCATION SHEET - DAY 1

1
10
-8
7R/30

7
6
+1
15R/28

13
8
-7
9M/32

2
6
-7
7L/28

8
9
-2
11L/26

14
11
-15
8M/46

3
16
-7
11M/36

9
8
-4
15R/38

15
7
-8
9L/34

4
8
-8
7M/30

10
7
-8
11M/38

16
5
+10
26L/32

5
7
-8
7M/30

11
4
-8
9L/34

17
13
-1
11M/24

6
6
+11
30L/38

12
8
+5
25R/40

18
7
-6
9M/30

Choosing Your Committee

As chairman you have the responsibility of selecting a committee of three or four people that you know you can work with and who will be responsible for their assigned tasks.

Select people who have abilities in the direction that you need. Special talents such as art, decorating, computer savvy and other skills will prove to be invaluable. A willingness to go "above and beyond" in the execution of their job will make yours, as chairman much easier. Enthusiasm for the project is essential. Depending upon the size of the tournament 3 or 4 committee members should suffice. Some projects are best done with the combined effort of all committee members. But at the first meeting it may be wise to assign a job to each person to research or develop before the next meeting. After selecting a theme, ordering prizes and favors should be a priority. A weekly meeting or more often, if necessary should be scheduled.

Evaluation and Reports
An overview critique of how things were handled and suggestions for improvements, are invaluable to succeeding chairpersons.

Soon after the tournament has ended it is important to gather all the records of expenses, how the tournament was run and received, to make a report for future chairperson's reference. There should be a manual or folder specific to the tournament that can be passed on to the next chairperson.

Favors
It has become customary to present all participants with a gift, that they may remember their outing, even if they do not win a major prize. The value of these favors, more or less, depend on the budget. If the budget is tight, only guests can be gifted. But it is best if all players receive a favor.

Selecting the favors from your prize vendor will sweeten the pot for a discount, giving you more purchasing power. Favors can be given at the registration table as the guests and members check in, or placed on the table at one of the meals. These add a nice touch if they are wrapped.

Mulligans

As part of choosing the format for the tournament, the committee should make a decision whether or not to allow mulligans. A mulligan is given or purchased by each member of the team and may be used at any time during the play. The decision must be made by the player when to use his mulligan during his turn. In the case of a two day tournament, mulligans can be given for each day, but not carried over.

Table Decorations

These can be simple or as elaborate as the committee chooses. Seasonal flowers put together by the committee are often lovely and allow the monies that would be spent on professional arrangements to be added to the prize budget. Keeping in tune with the theme can sometimes create a whimsical and creative decoration. One thought - lower arrangements, make for better interaction among guests rather than tall ones that block the view of your meal partners. Alternatively, high pilsner type vases with a few flowers can be equally effective and create the same ambiance. Plants or fruits and vegetables, a figurine, or centerpiece unique to the tournament theme are also good ideas. Color adds a great deal to any table setting, so consider bright fresh colors in table linens. Napkins can be tied with ribbon or raffia or bright yarn, further adding to the décor.

First choose your theme and develop your tournament plans from there. The chapter on theme suggestions should be most helpful.

Invitations

See the chapter on invitations for ideas, samples and suggestions.

Prizes

Selections and purchasing prizes and favors, should top your priority list. These may take some time to acquire and should be done promptly. See the chapter on prizes for suggestions on purchasing and displaying prizes.

Food and Beverage Service

Meeting with the club manager, assistant manager and chef are a necessary part of the tournament planning. Rely on their expertise to guide you.

Things to discuss and consider:

Cost
The exact number of meals to be served.

Will the type of food be in keeping with the theme of the event?

What type of food can be provided to stay within the budget?

Smaller tournaments or guest days try to be self supporting. Larger events, such as invitationals, may be partially subsidized by the club.

Menus
Type of service—plated or buffet?

Will there be an open bar or will it be a signature bar?

In what rooms will the meals be served?

Snacks on the golf course—traveling wagon or at specific locations?

Will the service people be costumed to follow the theme of the event?

Discuss the type of flowers or centerpieces.

Determine if there will be decorations in the locker rooms and restrooms on the golf course.

Make certain that the on course facilities are clean and well supplied. Provide an attendant in the locker rooms to handle shoe service or other requirements of the guests.

Will there be a band or music?

Will there be valet parking?

FOOD & BEVERAGE FUNCTION SHEET

DATE OF FUNCTION: **OCTOBER 15**   TIME: **11:00**   DAY: **THURSDAY**

TYPE OF FUNCTION: **PETERBILT GOLF OUTING**

MENU:

COCKTAIL SUPPER AT COMPLETION OF PLAY

STANDING RIB BEEF (SLICED AND SERVED ON HOMEMADE PETITE ROLLS)

HICKORY SMOKED HAM (SLICED AND SERVED ON HOMEMADE PETITE ROLLS)

SHRIMP SCAMPI

SWEDISH MEATBALLS

CHEF'S SPECIAL CHEESE BALL & CRACKERS

RELISH TRAY

CELERY W/CHEESE FILLING

STRAWBERRIES WITH CARAMEL SAUCE

ICED TEA

COFFEE

COST: $10.75 PER PERSON (PLUS TAX & GRATUITY)

BEVERAGE/BAR/BEER: (specifics)
TIME:

Premium Brand:	$4.75 per Drink
Call Brand:	$4.25 per Drink
Bar Brand:	$3.75 per Drink
House Wine:	$3.50 pre Glass
Domestic Beer:	$2.50 each
Imported Beer:	$3.00 each

SPECIAL INSTRUCTIONS:

NUMBER OF PEOPLE GUARANTEED: **125** X PRICE PER PERSON $ **13.39** = $ **$1673.75**
(including gratuity & state tax)

ROOM RENTAL: $400.00 + SALES TAX: $ **0** + SERVICE CHARGE $ = $ **0**

CHARGES FOR SPECIAL REQUIREMENTS: $

DEPOSIT DUE DATE ___ (Less Deposit) $

BALANCE DUE DATE ___ AMOUNT DUE $ **$1673.75**

POLICIES / REGULATIONS

*PAIRINGS MUST BE SUBMITTED 48 HOURS PRIOR TO TEE TIME. * TEE ASSIGNMENTS WILL ME MADE BY THE GOLF PROFESSIONAL. * IT IS REQUIRED THAT PRIZES BE PURCHASED THROUGH OUR PRO SHOPPE. * ALL FOOD & BEVERAGE MUST BE PURCHASED AND SERVED BY THE CLUB. * ORGANIZATIONS AGREE THAT THE MINIMUM CHARGE FOR FOOD WILL BE BASED ON THE NUMBER OF PEOPLE GUARANTEED 48 HOURS PRIOR TO THE FUNCTION. THE CLUB WILL BE PREPARED TO SERVE UP TO 10% IN EXCESS OF THE GUARANTEED NUMBER. * DRESS CODE: ALL MEN MUST WEAR SHIRTS WITH COLLARS. NO SHORT SHORTS OR BLUE JEANS PERMITTED. * GOLF CARTS MUST REMAIN ON THE CART PATHS AT ALL TIMES.

ANY CHANGES REGARDING THE ABOVE ARRANGEMENTS PRIOR TO 48 HOURS OF THE EVENT MUST BE MADE IN WRITING AND SIGNED BY AN AUTHORIZED AGENT OF THE ORGANIZATION & ACKNOWLEDGED BY THE CLUB.

The **PETERBILT GOLF OUTING** organization agrees to abide by the rules and regulations of NASHVILLE GOLF AND ATHLETIC CLUB and to pay for any damages caused by their group.

SIGNATURE: ___ DATE **10/15/98**

NASHVILLE GOLF & ATHLETIC CLUB

Formats

Format For Tournament Play

The following formats are taken from the PGA of America tournament book, with their permission. Work with your golf professional to select a format and he or she, will be glad to assist you in planning the event.

Match Play

Match play is an old form of golf. It is fun and exciting. You start each match even with your opponent. Match play can produce some unexpected victors, which is one of the things that make it fun.

Match play requires qualifying for entrance and positions, match play begins. Sixty-four players in a field after one round reduces the size of the field by one-half to thirty-two then 16-8-4-2 and finally one. On some occasions a consolation flight is offered. That is, the players who lose in the first round go into a tournament of their own. They maintain their respective positions in the flights and their field is also cut in half after each round until there is a winner.

Stroke Play

Most stroke play events are 18 hole one day events that produce a clear winner. In case of a tie, a sudden death, one hole (or more) play off will decide the winner.

One Day Events

Most golf events are one day stroke play events. These include:
36 hole stroke play tournaments
27 hole stroke play tournaments
18 hole stroke play
9 hole stroke play
Match play with stroke play qualifier
Match play with 9,18, or 36 hole formats

Multi-Day Events

Many tournaments are conducted over a period of days, usually two to four days. This is usually done because the contestants come from a considerable distance or because other entertainment is offered.

72 Hole Stroke Play
54 Hole stroke play
36 Hole stroke play
Match play events
Combination stroke play and match play event

Handicap Events
Handicaps are the equalizers in golf, be it a big multi-day event or a Saturday morning match. USGA type handicaps based on course ratings or the newer slope system, are very fair and when properly used will make any two players near equal on the first tee. Based on the USGA formula, you can give a person a legitimate handicap immediately.

Special Tournaments

Approach and Putting Contests
Each contestant approaches and holes out three balls from 25, 50 and 100 yards off the green. In each case each ball should be played from a different direction. The winner is the one holing out the three balls in the fewest number of strokes.

Best Ball of Three
This is not used as frequently as four-ball events, but still is interesting. A good mixed event two men and one woman, or visa-versa.

Best Ball of Four
Four players are a team, ideally a class A.B.C.D. Eighty percent of each player's handicap should be used, but some clubs use full handicaps. Golfers apply their handicap strokes to each hole and the lowest net score on each hole is recorded as the team score.

Better Ball of Partners (four ball)
Two players are a team. They apply their handicaps on the appropriate holes and have a net better ball on each hole, comprising the team score. Eighteen hole stroke play events are well liked. In many areas, only ninety percent of handicaps are used in Four Ball tournaments. Thirty-six hole events or events or 54 and 72 holes are all popular using this format.

Best Ball of Group Variation
A four man team event. One best ball is used on par five holes, two best balls on par four holes, and three on par three holes.

Blind Partners

This is an 18 hole stroke play round with 90 percent handicaps. Players may play the round with anyone of their choice. But partners are not drawn until the last group has teed off, so a player does not know his partner until he has finished. Winner is the team with lowest better ball score.

Blind Holes Tournament

The winning score is based on only nine holes, selected individually from among the 18 to be played. The holes are not selected until after all players have left the first tee, so that the players have no knowledge of the holes that will count, until they have finished play. Half handicap usually is used to compile net totals.

Bridgeman Best Ball of Foursome

Four players are a team using full handicaps. The eighteen hole record is divided into three six hole segments. Applying handicap strokes to each hole, the players use the one net best ball per hole on the first six holes, two net best balls on the second six holes and three net best balls on the final holes. As an option, all four net scores may be required on the last hole.

Best and Better Ball Events

Probably the type of event most enjoyed by the average golfer is the best ball or better ball type of format. Better ball of partners, or best ball of four or two best balls of four keeps everyone in the running and is a team effort.

Closest to the Line

A white chalk line is painted down the center of the fairway. Whoever hits the ball closest to the line is the winner.

Choice Nines of Partners

Partners play and select the best combination of one player's front nine and the other player's back nine. You can play this event as choice nines of the twosome, and combination. The same player's score may be used on the front and back nine.

Choice Nine on Front Nine, Better Ball on Back

A two player team selects one of the partner's front nine net score using half the handicap. The lowest front nine score combined with the net better ball of the pair combine to make an interesting game.

Long Drive Contest

A prize is awarded for the longest drive in your own fairway on one or two holes. In a two day guest tournament, offer prizes for guests and members, and change the holes each day.

Daily Sweepstake

On a given day, allow all players to enter a Sweepstakes. Prizes are awarded for the following: Eighteen holes—low gross. Eighteen holes—low net, first nine holes low gross, first nine—low net second nine holes—low gross second nine low net and fewest putts.

Deuces

On a given day in conjunction with another event Deuces can be an added event. Any natural two is a winner. No handicaps are used.

Eighteen Hole Throw Out

Players apply handicaps on the appropriate holes, then throw out three worst net scores.

Four Ball Stroke Play

Players are paired in two player teams and their better ball on each hole is the team score. Allow each player 90% of his handicap, the strokes taken as they appear on the card.

Four Ball Match Play vs. Par

Allow each player 90 percent of his full handicap, the strokes to be taken as they come on the card. (When a player has a plus handicap, Par is allowed 90 percent of the player's plus handicap.)

Flag Tournament

Players are given a small flag with their names attached to the flagstick. Using full handicap, play until reaching the number of strokes equaling par, plus handicap. The flag is planted after using the quota of strokes, playing an extra hole or two if necessary. The winner is the player who plants the flag farthest around the course. Variation is to award equal prizes to all players who hole out at the 18th green within their allotted number of strokes. THE UNITED STATES FLAG SHOULD NEVER BE USED AS A MARKER IN SUCH TOURNAMENTS

Fewest Putts

This is a gross tournament. Players keep track of all shots made from the putting surface. Only strokes take with a putter on the putting surface are counted. No handicaps are used. The winner is the player using the fewest putts.

Gross Minus Putts

All players keep track of putts and subtract these from their score at the end of the round. This should be a gross event.

Handicap Stroke Play

Players play 18 holes of stroke play. Prizes may be awarded for best gross and net scores. Full handicaps are used.

Mixed Foursomes

These are a Sunday afternoon standard feature at many clubs, and they are now played in three ways, The official way is for the partners to alternate driving from each tee and then to play alternate shots until the ball is holed. The second way is perhaps more enjoyable for average golfers with both partners driving from each tee and selecting which ball to play thereafter. A third method was introduced by Mr. and Mrs. Chapman with interesting results. Both partners drive from each tee, and then each plays a second shot with the other's ball. After second shots choose the ball with which the hole will be completed, alternate shots being continued.

Two Low Balls of Foursome With Each Person Having to Play at Least Eight Holes.

Using full handicaps, four players record the two best net scores on each hole. The catch is that each player must use his score a minimum of eight times during the round. You must insist that players mark down all four scores and select the two scores that are to be used at the completion of every hole and may not be changed.

Most 3's, 4's, and 5's

Players use full handicap, taking the strokes as they fall on the card. Prizes are awarded to the players scoring the most net 3's, 4's and 5's.

Match Play vs. Bogey

A good ladies event. Using the correct application of handicaps, each player plays a match against bogey. The player with the greatest lead against par is the winner of this event.

Match Play of Team Total

A two player team event. Seed teams into match play, or have qualifying. The match play will be played by team net total on each hole. Apply handicaps appropriately to handicap holes.

Nassau Tournament

This is similar to the handicap stroke play except that handicap strokes are taken hole-by-hole as they fall on the card and prizes are awarded for best first nine, best second nine, and the best 18 holes. The advantage is that a player making a poor start, or tiring at the finish, may still win a prize for his play on the other nine.

Point System Team Style

Using the handicaps, each player on each hole is awarded one point for a net bogey, two points for a net par, three points for a net birdie.

Scrambles

Scrambles are probably the most fun for people to play because you only play the good shots. For a basic format: four man teams are put together, preferably A,B,C,D, class players. All players drive from the tee and select the best shot. All players then play the next shot from the position of the selected ball, placing or dropping their ball within an agreed on distance i.e. one foot or a club length from that spot. The same procedure is used on all shots, including putts. Some formats use a rule that if the chosen ball is in the rough or a bunker or water hazard, the designated one foot or one club length distance must also be the in rough or hazard Also when selecting a ball to be played on the fringe, the other balls must be played from the fringe. This is a gross event. Handicaps are difficult to apply but the best method is to use thirty percent of the lowest player's handicap, or 10% of the combined handicap of the group.

Having players of varying handicaps play from different tees, allows players of all caliber feel they are a part of the team. A high-handicap player can then be as much of an asset as a low-handicap player. A variation requires that every player's tee shot must be used at least three or possibly four times. Another format is that if any given player's shot is selected he may not play on the next shot. These additions can tend to equalize teams that may have exceptionally strong players on them.

One or two best ball ringer tournament.

This is a favorite of the ladies and can be applied to a guest day. If the tournament is a one day event, use one best ball of the team. Use full handicap with a maximum of 36.

In the case of a two day event the second day the scores may be bettered to arrive at the best ball. This format may be played one or two best balls. This format may also be referred to as Selected Score.

Two Best Balls of Four Using One Gross and One Net score on Each Hole
The four-man team must use one gross and one net score on each hole. The same player's ball may not be used for both.

Three Best Balls of Four
A four-man team using full handicaps finds the three best net scores per hole, adds them up and that becomes the team score.

Two Man Mixed Bag Multi Day Event
Two Man Mixed Bag Multi Day thirty-six hole two man event is interesting and challenging if it is broken down into four nine-hole stroke play events, with all scores totaled. The first nine should be best ball, the second nine a Chapman System and alternate shots the third.

Hole-In-One

Hole-in-One

Provisions should be made for a Hole-In-One Award. It can happen!!

In an important tournament like an Invitational, big ticket items can be awarded, such as cars, jewelry, or trips. The budget usually does not cover this, so the club buys insurance to cover the expense if the prize is won. Your pro shop can work with you on obtaining this insurance.

If the tournament is a one day event, usually the groups' treasury can offer a monetary award either in cash or in merchandise in the pro shop.

Trophies are also available denoting this accomplishment.

REPUBLIC UNDERWRITERS INSURANCE COMPANY	Endorsement No. __1__ Effective Date 07/19/01-07/20/01
	Certificate No. _____ 301472 _____
	To Policy No._____ 10194200M _____

consideration of the fee paid, the certificate is amended as follows:

1. You are allowed, under this certificate and in conjunction with this insured tournament, to have a Putting event with the following terms:

DURING THE EVENT:

A. PUTTING EVENT CONDITIONS -
   - Contestants: One Amateur
   - Putts: one putt attempt
   - Distance: 50 feet
   - Prize value: $2,500
   - Prize Description: Cash

B. ELIGIBILITY - One amateur contestant that must be an officially registered and qualified contestant of the insured tournament.

C. WITNESSES: One witness must observe at the cup and be a non-participant of the insured tournament, age 18 or over, of good moral character, and appointed by the Association member.

D. PUTT: A putt is defined as a "stroke" by the USGA Rules of Golf. Once a putt passes the target hole, it becomes ineligible. ONLY one putt is permitted. No practice putts, mulligans, or substituted putts are permitted. The authorized putt is permitted only during the stipulated contest of the named event on the date agreed upon.

E. TARGET HOLE - Only one target hole is allowed for this contest. The target hole must be USGA official size in the putting surface. Cup placement will not be permitted in a concave area of the putting green. No blocking or grooving of a path to the target hole to improve the chances of a holed putt shall be permitted.

F. PUTTING GREEN - Only natural turf greens are permitted.

G. VARIABLE EVENT CONDITIONS - No changes are allowed to these conditions.

By _____
        Authorized Representative

NATIONAL HOLE-IN-ONE ASSOCIATION

DALLAS · LONDON

HOLE-IN-ONE PROGRAM

CERTIFICATE OF PARTICIPATION

CERTIFICATE #301472
**Amendment #A1

INSURED MEMBER'S NAME: Finishline Ford Lincoln Mercury

TOURNAMENT DATE(S): 07/19/01 - 07/20/01

NAME OF EVENT: Elk River Men's Invitational
LOCATION OF EVENT: Elk River

TARGET HOLE CONTESTANTS:

Amateurs	Club Pros	Tour Pros	Total Shots
264	0	0	264

HOLE #	YARDAGE**	PRIZE VALUE	DESCRIPTION
#15	171	$65,000	2001 Toyota Sequoia
#12	169	Sony View-Camcorder	

TOTAL CERTIFICATE FEE: $3,433.00

Ladies allowed to use forward tees per course score card.

CAUTION
Target Hole(s) and prize
must be offered on
Exact Hole(s)
as shown on this certificate
Read Condition B-6 carefully.

MEMBERSHIP BONUS:
· Personalized Color Sign For Sponsor's Target Hole

The NATIONAL HOLE-IN-ONE ASSOCIATION, of Dallas, Texas, who issued this Certificate of Participation is the named insured under Master Policy #100194200M issued by Republic Underwriters Insurance Company insuring NHIOA's obligations for the exclusive benefit of the association member named above.

Date Issued:

NATIONAL HOLE-IN-ONE ASSOCIATION

July 20, 2001

11910 Greenville Avenue • Fourth Floor • Dallas, Texas 75243-9364
U.S. and Canada 1-(800) 527-6944 • Dallas (972) 808-9001 • FAX (972) 808-9012

Douglas J Burkert, President

33

Invitations

Invitations

Special invitations are most often used during an invitational tournament, and are mailed out to guests from the pro-shop.

These invitations can be printed outside or created on the computer.

There are several greeting card workshop software programs available. These include clip art and readily enable a creative person to customize the invitation to match the theme of the tournament. They can be made in any size, half-fold, quarter-fold, postcard or in the form of a flyer. Samples of each follow.

Invitations that are not mailed out can be made accessible in the locker rooms or in the pro-shop for the member to pick up and mail to his or her guest.

Programs that may be helpful are:
American Greetings CreataCard
Microsoft Greetings Workshop
Microsoft Works
Publishers Printshop

Entry Form

(Member's) Name   _____

Club Acct. #   _____

1. (Guest's) Name   _____

    Phone #   _____

    Golf Club   _____

    Club Phone #   _____

    Guest Index   _____

    Guest Handicap   _____

2. (Guest's) Name   _____

    Phone #   _____

    Golf Club   _____

    Club Phone #   _____

    Guest Index   _____

    Guest Handicap   _____

3. (Guest's) Name   _____

    Phone #   _____

    Golf Club   _____

    Club Phone #   _____

    Guest Index   _____

    Guest Handicap   _____

Please fill-out the above form and mail or fax it back to Golf Shop by _____ (date). Fax # ( ) _____

If sizes are necessary for favors, the request for same may be included in this form.

Flyer

.Rolling Meadows Golf Club

SAMPLE

Y̶ ̶̶ ̶̶ to play in our
Inv̶ ̶̶nal on June 21 and 22.
9:00 shotgun both days
Continental Breakfast and
luncheon both days
Practice round June available on
June 20.
Call the pro shop for details.
898-9779

Quarter-Fold

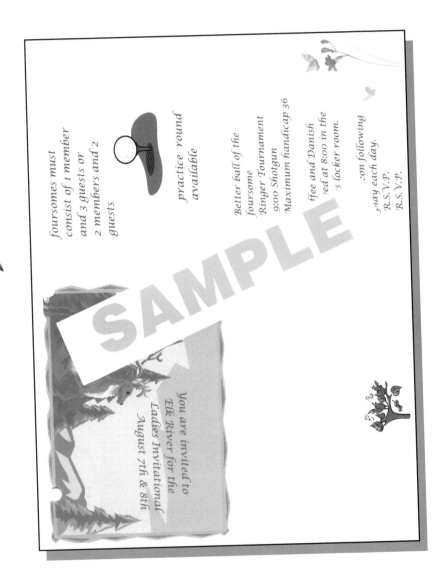

foursomes must consist of 1 member and 3 guests or 2 members and 2 guests

practice round available

Better ball of the foursome
Ringer Tournament
9:00 Shotgun
Maximum handicap 36

ffee and Danish
'ed at 8:00 in the
's locker room.

:on following
.nay each day.
R.S.V.P.
R.S.V.P.

You are invited to
Elk River for the
Ladies Invitational
August 7th & 8th

SAMPLE

Half-Fold

ne *World* in *18 Holes!!*

Half-Fold

Golf, cocktails and Dinner
Wednesday May 10th
1:00 shotgun
Inverness Golf Club
R.S.V.P.

Mulligans

Mulligans

Mulligans give the players a second chance to improve a shot and therefore improve the score. They are used at the discretion of the team and usually the opinion of the stronger player on the team is respected. They may be used at any time including on the putting green, but must be declared immediately if they are to replace a shot. The best strategy for the use of a mulligan is very frequently on the putting green.

Mulligans are sometimes offered for purchase at the registration table. Often they are given to each player on the team, which I think proves to be the better choice. Mulligans can be presented in the form of ribbons or stickers in keeping with the theme.

Photographs

Photographs

If the committee agrees, select someone to take photographs of the members and their guests. This is most conveniently pro-shop staff or someone who is not playing in the tournament. A professional photographer could also be used, especially for large invitational tournaments, if the budget permits. Photographs take from the waist up, are more easily recognizable and flattering to the participants. These photographs are often displayed at luncheon or dinner place settings.

Posting the photographs on a scoreboard is most effective and usually well received by all, and makes a very nice presentation, allowing people to get to know each other better.

Prizes

Prizes

Prizes should be in keeping with the theme of the tournament and displayed on a suitably draped and skirted table. They should be labeled according to flights and as first, second and third, net and gross, depending on how many places you are going to recognize. Also you would have closest to the pin and longest drive or closest to the line prizes. Printing the signs or labels in calligraphy creates a nice appearance. The table should also be adorned with a flower arrangement, plants and ribbons to make it attractive. Purchasing prizes from a local merchant will create good will and usually the merchant will offer a discount for a large order. You may also be able to avoid shipping charges by shopping locally.

If the tournament is more than one day, especially for corporate outings or club invitationals, it is appropriate to present the guests with a tee prize each day. A few suggestions are: logoed club glassware, wind shirts or vests, golf balls, watches that attach to the golf bag.

Putting Contest

Putting Contest

Preparing a contest on the putting green can be most creative. Usually nine holes are outlined with string and push pins. The "fairways" can be decorated with sand, stones, and twigs. Other obstacles, such as plastic buildings, mountains, and tunnels can also be used. Stuffed or plastic animals also add to the fun. It is appropriate to go with the theme of the tournament.

Players are encouraged to participate either before the tournament starts, after the daily play, or even if waiting for their position in the tee box. A one dollar entry fee can be collected by the person overseeing the contest, and the monies taken in are awarded to the player with the least number of putts. A contestant may enter as often as he likes. Usually an assistant from the pro shop supervises the contest and keeps a record of the players and the monies collected. You may opt to award a special prize for the winner of the putting contest in lieu of collecting an entry fee.

Sign up Sheet

A sign up sheet should be available in the pro-shop at least one month before the tournament for members to enter their guest's name, home club, and handicap or index.

Entry forms could also be mailed to members that will include the aforementioned information. These then can be turned into the pro-shop. A sign up sheet is also often posted in the locker rooms.

Most tournaments limit the number of participants according to what the club, and course/courses can accomodate. There is usually a cut off time for accepting entries. This should be posted on the sign up sheet and stated on the initial mailing from the pro-shop.

Themes

Themes

A great basis for planning a tournament begins with selecting a theme. There is a multitude of ideas out there just waiting to be developed. The choice depends on who the tournament is for—whether it be a ladies', men's or mixed event. The location of the tournament and the time of year are also a consideration.

Seasonal or holiday themes are a natural for invitations, decorations, prizes and food selections.

Just how far you can develop a theme depends primarily on your budget, your committee and your imagination. Usually there is a vast treasure house of talent within club members and staff. Ferret out these talents and use them!

The computer offers alot of free clip art to use for invitations, flyers and pre-tournament hype. Enlist the help of a computer literate person who will be flattered to be of assistance.

The following pages will list types of themes and suggestions for carrying them out. Remember these do not have to be elaborate. The use of readily available items (i.e. seasonal flowers) can be just as effective if done in good taste.

A good website to check out for help with numerous theme based events is: www.themepartiesnmore.com

Around the World Theme

Around the World in 18 Holes

Invitations
This is really a fun tournament and is well used for all types of tournaments. Men's, Ladies or Mixed. Invitations could have a hot air balloon on the cover page. At registration you could have a tape playing the title song Around the World in Eighty Days.

Decorations
Table decorations could be different each day if the event was more than one day. Use decorations indigenous to the various countries you represent. Flags work well, or hats or costume accessories from the different countries. Posters from travel agencies are colorful and would add to the decor.

Favors
Travel or tote bags with the club logo.

Menu
The best way to serve the meals because of the variety of items is with a buffet, featuring stations with food from different countries. Suggestions are: American, French, German, Mexican, Moroccan, Oriental, and Scandinavian.

Menu possibilities are: bratwurst, chicken and couscous, crepes, pasta, quesadillas, sweet and sour pork. A luncheon could be an American barbeque with hamburgers, baked beans and apple pie.

Half way food stations could have (as for Morocco) trail mix, dates, baskets of fruit, and cold drinks. An attendant dressed in a long Moroccan robe and wearing a fez is your server. Also there can be a cheese table representing Holland with the attendant dressed in native costume. The pro-shop staff should be appropriately dressed internationally, in kilts, lederhosen, oriental garb, Nordic headdresses, Chinese beanie with a braid, French beret, or Hawaiian garb.

Formats
If it is a two day tournament do 2 best balls of the foursome net and gross with 90% handicap. For a one day tournament one best ball, or better ball of partners. Have Mulligans.

Prizes
Prizes could be gifts from the various countries. Food baskets or products pertaining to the specific countries: wine, chocolate, trays, dishes. pottery. Also international cook books make a nice gift. Other possibilities are clothing, accessories, leather goods, silk scarves, photograph albums, picture frames.

A Hole-in-One prize : a trip for two to some overseas location.

Australian Theme

Australian Outback Theme

This is a good men's tournament

Invitations
Kangaroos and boomerangs
Start with G'Day, Join me "down under"

Decorations
Centerpiece: Bamboo stalks with koala bears
Leather Hats, Boomerangs, Kangaroo, Koala bears
Brown napkins tied with rawhide
Travel posters of Australia

Favors
Barbecue fork
Key chains
Leather prospector hats

Menu
Baby lamb chops for appetizers.   Bloomin' onion
Make a menu like the Outback Restaurant. They might even be willing to cater it.
Chicken and Ribs on the "Barbie",
Cocoanut shrimp, Aussie fries,
Chunky Bread
Salad bar
Dessert: Make your own sundaes or
Tasmanian devil's-food cake with ice cream *(See recipe index)*

Format
Five nine hole matches, flighted. Winners to play off for overall winner. Flights named with Australian things—koalas, 'roos, kookaburras, dingoes, platypus, etc.

Prizes
Case of Australian wine
Things made of Merino wool
Opals, gold nuggets
Magnetic copper bracelets

This could be a great theme for a fantastic putting green decorated with crocodiles, platypus, koalas, bamboo, butterflies, insects, miniature prospecting tools, burlap bags of sand representing ores. Fish, crabs, lobster representing the Great Barrier Reef.

Hole-in-one prize
Round trip to Australia

Bugs and Butterflies Theme

Bugs and Butterflies

Invitations
All manner of bug and butterfly clip art or stationery is available. On the invitation a nice thought to include is: *Happiness is like a butterfly*. The more you chase it, the more it will elude you. But if you turn your attention to other things it will settle on your shoulder.

Decorations
Flowers and bugs and butterflies

Favors
Can be anything that goes with the theme. Perhaps a garden"bug or butterfly"

Menu
A spring luncheon with fresh flavors and color
Nectarine chicken salad
Croissant
Lemon Mousse for dessert

Format
3-3-3-
Use the score of 3 best par 3's
3 best par 4's
3 best par 5's
Bug and Butterfly stickers for Mulligans

Prizes
Dishes, stationery, English placemats, playing cards
Ornamental boxes with bugs and butterflies. Garden accessories.

Candlelight and Roses Theme

Candlelight and Roses Theme

Invitations
Light up my life and be my guest for our candlelight and roses tournament. Pictures of candles, hurricane lamps, roses

Decorations
Candelabra centerpieces or hurricane shades in floral arrangements
Roses

Favors
Travel candles which are wrapped in gossamer fabric, jewels strewn on the table. Crystal votive candle holders. Metal votive candles, Miniature flashlights and book lights, are other suggestions .

Menu
Watercress soup
Poached salmon on a bed of greens with aioli dressing.
Salad of citrus on bib lettuce with citrus dressing.

Dessert
Individual berry cobbler with sugar cookie crust.

Format
Nine hole scramble first nine, Best ball second nine.

Prizes
Bud vases, candles, flower of the month gift certificate.
Candlesticks, Candle rings, Candle snuffers, Glass birthday candle holders. Oil candlesticks or lamps.

Christmas Theme

Christmas Theme

Invitations
Any type of Christmas artwork can be used. Holly, Santas, Ornaments

Decorations
Centerpiece:
Apple Christmas trees, made on a form surrounded with ever-greens.
(Instructions for constructing these on last page of this chapter.)
Napkins of red or green, or white tied with red and green yarn or ribbon
Evergreen boughs
Ask pro-shop staff to wear red or green shirts and Santa Hats.

Favors
Christmas ornaments

Menu
Red molded cranberry salad
Turkey casserole with fresh vegetables
Alternatively, cranberry chicken with green salad
Plum pudding with hard sauce for dessert

Format
One best ball on the par fives, two best balls on the par fours and three best balls on the par threes. Full handicap with a maximum of 36.

Prizes
All things Christmas. Wonderful Santas, dishes, angels, snow babies, linens are great prizes.
Decorate prize table with evergreens and red and green ribbons and poinsettias if they are available. Christmas cactus could also be used.

Colonial Apple Tree

List of materials
3 ¼" diameter dowels (each 48" long)
1 - 12" long piece of 1 ½" diameter dowel
¾" thick stock pine board for base
wood glue
1 - 1 ½" wood screw

Cut the ¼" dowels in the following quantities and lengths:

8 - 4 ½" pieces for the lowest row
6 - 4" pieces for the next row up
6 - 3 ½" pieces for the next row up
6 - 3" pieces for the next row up
1 - 2" piece for the top

All of these pieces were sharpened on one end with a hand held pencil sharpener. The other end was rounded slightly with the sharpener to allow for ease of assembly.

The 1 ½" diameter dowel was drilled with ½" holes to a depth of ¼" at the following measurements, starting at the bottom of the dowel where it attaches to the base and measuring up: (see tree form for the offset of the holes).

• 8 holes, evenly spaced, at 2 ⅛" from the bottom of the dowel
• 6 holes, evenly spaced, at 5" from the bottom of the dowel, offset from the row below
• 6 holes, evenly spaced, at 7 ¼" from the bottom of the dowel, offset from the row below
• 6 holes, evenly spaced, at 10" from the bottom of the dowel, offset from the row below
• 1 hole, centered, in the top of the dowel

The base was cut in 1 ½" x 10 ¼" strips of ¾" pine board stock, with the 10 ¼" dimension running with the grain of the wood. The ends were beveled at a 45 degree angle, and the midsections were carved out ⅜" deep to interlock the two strips using a table saw. A small, countersunk hole was drilled through the interlocked base pieces and the center of the bottom of the large dowel to start the wood-screw.

To assemble, the base was screwed to the bottom of the large dowel. Then the slightly rounded ends of the ¼" dowels were dipped into wood glue and pushed into the holes, starting with the longest dowels (8) nearest the base and progressing towards the 2" dowel in the top.

It takes about an hour to cut and make one form. This process would go much faster if done assembly-line style for cutting and assembly.

Colonial Apple Tree

Materials
Apple tree form
2½ dozen apples
1 small pineapple (optional) or a pillar candle
Greens (any combination of evergreens, boxwood, yew, holly, laurel)
1 small tray

Method
Soak greens in water 2-3 hours.
Shine apples.
Place tree form on tray.
Start placing apples, stem end up, on the bottom row of sticks.
Continue until all sticks have apples on them.
Place either a small pineapple or a perfect apple on top. (A pillar candle also can be used.)
Start at bottom and fill in all empty spaces with the greens. A combination of boxwood and holly makes a very pretty tree.

Variations
A collar of magnolia leaves or holly can be used around the base. For other holidays, lemons, oranges, or a combination of both may be used.

The tree will last one week. The life may be prolonged by putting the tree in a cool place each night.

Country Theme

Appalachian Country Theme

Invitations
Depict cloggers, mountains, quilt patterns, pottery

Decorations
Centerpiece: a burlap square or a calico print on table with bouquets of daisies in a crock. Rhododendrons could also be used. Assorted colored napkins tied with ribbon or rick- rack. Possibly you could obtain a dulcimer player to provide music during or before lunch.

Favors
Pottery pieces that are hand thrown in the mountains

Format
One best ball of partner's net and gross.
(eliminate one hole on the front side (gone fishin') and one hole on the back side(gone huntin')

Menu
Serve buffet style:
Fried chicken or BBQ Pork
Sausage gravy with biscuits
Cold Slaw
Green beans
Fruit cobbler for dessert

Prizes
Appalachian pottery,
Woven placemats or blankets
Baskets
Paintings of mountain scenery
Have quilt for a door prize. Give out raffle tickets at registration

Mulligans
Quilt squares

Easter Theme

Easter Theme

Invitations: Bunnies, Easter Eggs, Chickens
(Hop on over to our club for the Easter Parade)

Decorations
All things Easter, Pastel colors, Pink, Purple, Yellows, and Blue
Centerpieces: Rabbits or baskets of colored eggs on a bed of "grass"
Jelly beans. Easter Lilies
Napkins in pastels tied with pastel ribbons.
Request that the pro-shop staff wear pastel shirts and khaki pants.

Menu
Spinach salad
Ham Quiche with fruit garnish
Dessert:
Coconut layer cake with lemon curd filling.

Favors
Crystal or china rabbits or eggs.

Format
Two best balls of the foursome

Mulligans
Rabbit or Easter Basket stickers

Prizes
Crystal, woven or ceramic baskets
Ceramic rabbits
Platters or dishes with rabbit motif (Arthur Court make a fabulous
one. These are pressed aluminum plates and accessories of good
quality, available in gift shops and department stores.)
Deviled egg dishes.

Garden Theme

Garden Theme

Invitations
Flowers, Herbs, Garden tools
This tournament works for the ladies.

Decorations
Centerpiece:
Small clay pots of herbs in a large clay saucer. One pot for each place at the table.
Packets of seeds
A square of burlap under the large saucer
Green Napkins tied with raffia
Tees decorated with plants or nosegay bouquets

Favors
Garden gloves

Menu
Vichyssoise
Cobb salads or Chicken Caesar Salad. Crusty bread
Strawberries and blueberries with sabayon sauce served in bubble wine glasses with a cookie

Format
Point tournament: 1 point for bogie, 2 points for par, 3 points for birdie and 4 points for eagle. Net with full handicap—maximum 36. Gross prizes should also be given.

Prizes
Garden statuary, garden tools, hose sprinkler head attachments, books on gardening, flower arranging, and herbs. Plants, Interesting containers. Garden wagon. Decorative door wreaths. Garden torches. Knee pads.
Straw hats.
English placemats of heavy board with flowers, coasters, garden journals, stationery, note paper.

Special prize for most often on the green in regulation. Value 5 points.

Prizes for the longest drive and closest to the line

Mulligans
Stickers of flowers.

Golf is for the Birdies
Theme

Golf is for the Birdies Theme

Invitations
Front page, birds of all kinds.
This tournament is suitable for a Ladies' Day.

Decorations
Centerpieces: bird houses to be given as a table prize. Displayed in a nest of straw.

Favors
Notepaper with birds on it, cocktail napkins, playing cards, or anything regarding the theme.

Menu
A chicken entrée perhaps served in a nest of angel hair pasta.
Vegetables, a salad and dessert.
A unique dessert is a nest of shredded fillo dough filled with "eggs" of different colored sorbet.

Format
One best ball of the foursome, with a special prize for the most birdies net and gross.

Longest drive and closest to the pin prizes for both guests and members.

Prizes
A variety of bird feeders displayed on the prize table with sunflowers and birdseed. Also bird books, carved wooden or ceramic birds, dishes, spreaders, trays, coasters all in keeping with the theme.

Halloween Theme

Halloween Theme

Invitations
Themed accordingly with pumpkins, ghosts, corn candy, witches, black cats.

Decorations
Centerpieces: pumpkins filled with flowers or carved pumpkins. Witches hats could also be used.
Have black cat flags on the pins.
Put "ghosts" in bunkers or on tee boxes.

Favors
Halloween candles.

Menu
Pumpkin soup
Ghost Toasties—Grilled ham and cheese sandwiches on rye bread.
Green salad with apple and raisins.
Black Cat chocolate brownie with ice cream.

Format
Best score on all par threes, gross and net, allowing no more than 2 strokes handicap per hole.
Throw out the thirteenth hole at the end of the tournament.

Prizes
Clay pottery pumpkins or other Halloween related things that hold candles.
Ceramic dishes that depict Halloween.

Hawaiian Theme

Hawaiian Theme

Invitations
Could feature tropical flowers, hula girls or volcanoes. This theme is suitable for Men's, Mixed or Ladies' tournaments. Suggest that guests try to dress to the theme.

Greet your guests with a traditional Hawaiian flower or paper lei. Golf shop employees can wear flowered shirts and white pants. Waitresses wear Hawaiian shirts and white slacks or shorts for daytime or muumuus with flowers in their hair for the dinner night.

Decorations
Should be bright and colorful, bright colored linens and tropical flower centerpieces. Effective decorations are mini volcanoes fashioned out of sand or plaster with sterno for the volcanoes. These can also be used on the putting green for the putting contest or as tee markers. Seashells, glass floats, fishnet, raffia table skirts, would all add to the theme. If the party can be held by the pool, so much the better. Tiki torches add a romantic, tropical atmosphere. Hawaiian troupes can be hired for a hula show and music. A hula contest for both ladies and men is a lot of fun.

Decorations can be ordered online at www.islandmadness.com

Favors
Glass hibiscus vase

Menu
A Ladies' luncheon entrée could be ½ a pineapple with chicken or seafood salad. Fruit bread is a nice accompaniment. A fruit parfait would make a wonderful dessert. For a mixed tournament create a Luau- a wonderful buffet table with ice carving and flowers. Roast pig is a forgone conclusion and could be the centerpiece of the buffet. One end of the buffet should be seafood or perhaps a separate table could be set up for it.

A dessert buffet should include, desserts made with cocoanut or pineapple. A bowl of fresh fruit would also be appropriate. An individual dessert of baked Alaska served at each table, makes a fine presentation at the conclusion of the meal.

Format

Best used in a mixed two day tournament. One day play nine holes best ball with opposite spouses as partners. Play a scramble fore the second nine. The second day play better one or two best balls of the foursome for the entire 18 holes.

Prizes

Glass dolphin figurines
Round trip tickets to Hawaii for two.
Orchid plants.
Coral or pearl jewelry

Invitational Tournament Theme

Invitational Tournaments

Invitational tournaments are usually the highlight of the golfing season and require a lot of coordination and planning. They last two or three days and require scheduling to entertain your guests.

Invitations are customarily sent out by the pro-shop and include a form for the guest to return that has his handicap and index, and sizes, if wind shirts or sweaters are to be given as favors. These should be mailed at least 1 month before the tournament.

The first day after the practice round a cocktail party with heavy hors d'oeuvres, perhaps given poolside is a nice kick off and social event.

The morning of the first day of the tournament a registration table is set up where players receive pairings and tee assignments. Favors are sometimes given at this time. A continental breakfast buffet is also offered.

Luncheon buffets are made available at the turn each day of the tournament.

An evening barbeque the first day of the tournament affords players the opportunity to become acquainted with the field. This is usually an early evening. Encourage guests to dress western casual. The menu for this evening should be chuck wagon fare, burgers, hot dogs, pulled pork, baked beans, cold slaw, and a cobbler or brownies for dessert.

A dinner dance is customary the evening of the final day of the tournament. Prizes can be awarded either at the pre-dinner cocktail party or following dinner. This evening's menu is usually a gourmet dinner, possibly beef tenderloin medallions, with a red wine sauce, potatoes Anna, and a vegetable. A presented salad and dessert, are included. Soup or seafood cocktail may also be served.

Entertainment during the day:
If this is a men's tournament, activities that can be planned for the ladies are; luncheon, home tours, fashion shows, trunk shows by local merchants, (clothing or jewelry), shopping trips, card games, or golf at a neighboring club.

Ladies also enjoy demonstrations of cosmetics, or food preparation. (perhaps a garnishing demonstration presented by the chef)

Having a licensed mental sports consultant and hypnotherapist present a program on Positive Mental Imaging is an informative, enlightening and entertaining experience. Men also enjoy this program.

I can personally endorse this program founded in 1992 by Joan King, CH, Master Sports Hypnotist. Joan's teaching credentials include a B.A. in Psychology from the University of Vermont and Adjunct Instructor at colleges in Ohio and Florida. She is a senior golfer who competes in national and international golf championships. You can contact Joan@pmi4@att.net. The men also enjoy golf clinics, professional golf demonstrations, putting contests.

Professional speakers can be found through the PGA of America. Golf psychologists often provide a helpful and entertaining program, reinforcing the mental side of the game.

Format
The men enjoy 9 hole matches with handicaps that are flighted. See format chapter as to how these matches are run. There is usually an overall winner, net and gross. Flights are given names, usually in keeping with the theme of the tournament.

A score board with partner's pictures add to the overall excitement, and is usually created by the pro-shop.

Often pari-mutual wagering is a large part of this tournament, and is offered at the welcome cocktail party. Both men and women guests are allowed to participate.

Prizes
Often logo prizes are awarded. Prizes can also be in keeping with a theme if there is one. Crystal, leather goods, i.e. photo albums, coasters, wine buckets, desk accessories are all good choices.

Hole-in-one prizes are important in this tournament and automobiles, or other sports vehicles, or equipment can be insured and offered to the winner.

Ladies' Invitational Tournaments
Ladies' invitational tournaments usually last two or three days, with the first day being a practice round. A format that appeals to the ladies is a ringer tournament, gross and net, where the first day scores, either one or two best balls of the foursome, or best ball of the twosome are recorded and can be improved upon in the following day.

Continental breakfast usually precedes both days of play. A salad bar luncheon works for the first day of the tournament, and a wine and cheese reception following play the second day with a sit down luncheon followed by the awarding of prizes.

Centerpieces are often given away and a fun way to do this is as follows. The tournament chairperson takes the mike to read The Centerpiece Game.

The Centerpiece Game
If you are the youngest sitting in a seat
Take the gift it will be your treat.

You have won me now, but you must share
Pass me to the left lady with the darkest hair.

Now's here's the test, measure them all
Give me to the girl who is the most tall.

I've had my turn with the tallest
Now give me to the one who's the smallest.

This may be mad, this may be foolery
Give me to the lady who's wearing the most jewelry.

Pass me along and turn your head
Give me to the lady who is most in red.

We're all so busy and in our car
Give me to the lady who's come the most far.

Of grandchildren we love to boast
Give me to the lady with the most.

Ashes to ashes, Dust to dust
Give me to the lady with the smallest bust.

This little game can go on night and day
Pass me to the left, two seats away.

Here I am no more to roam, I'm yours to keep
So — Please take me home!!

This little game is a lot of fun and will have your guests laughing and in good spirits. (Thanks to Glad Elting.)

Charity Tournaments

Often tournaments are given for charitable organizations as fund raisers. These tournaments can be patterned after the chapter on "Invitationals," using many of the same ideas.

Tournaments are given for the local chamber of commerce, animal rescue, children's homes, child abuse, research for disease, and a multitude of causes, local and national.

Frequently the cause involved will provide prizes and favors. For instance, Rally for the Cure which is a campaign for early detection of breast cancer is sponsored by Golf for Women Magazine. Fifty states and two foreign countries were represented in 2002. Men have also participated in this event. Participants are awarded the symbolic pink ribbon pin with a golf club, pink ribbon golf balls and each receive a subscription to Golf for Women Magazine. Other prizes are donated for closest to the pin contests. For more information regarding this tournament the web site is info@rallyforacure.com

Corporate Outings

Invitations to corporate outings are extended by the host and are usually printed. The expenses of the outing fall to the host and can be considerable, so the club must do its' utmost to carry out the hosts wishes to a tee! Forms are included in the written invitation listing participant's shirt, belt, and glove size for favor information. Favors could also include one dozen golf balls, or club visors.

The golf professional should work closely with the host in selecting new merchandise for prizes and have them ordered well in advance. Current or end of season merchandise is not acceptable. To encourage sales in the pro-shop the pro could offer a special sale to tournament participants.

The host usually provides lodging for the guests, transportation to the place of lodging and shuttle service to and from the club.

The outings frequently begin on a Wednesday with a practice round, followed by cocktails and dinner. Play begins Thursday afternoon. Thursday morning is spent in clinics. Luncheon is to be served both Thursday and Friday. Most men enjoy hamburgers or bratwurst or make your own sandwiches for luncheon.

An excellent choice of activity for the guests is to have their swing analyzed by a professional club fitter, such as Titlest or Callaway. Each guest would receive recommendations for the perfect club for his swing, and prizes might include a certificate for a custom made club according to their personalized club fitting.

A putting contest should be set up and available throughout the span of the tournament. *(See chapter on putting contests.)*

Thursday night cocktails and dinner, coat and tie required. Entertainment should include a professional speaker such as a golf psychologist, or someone who has written a book on the game of golf. In good taste "strippers" should not be considered as part of the entertainment.

Another round of 18 holes of golf is played on Friday. The conclusion of the tournament is Friday evening with cocktails and dinner, and the awarding of prizes.

Large prizes such as golf bags should be shipped to the recipient, if necessary.

Jungle Theme

Jungle Theme

Invitations
Animal Images. "Take a safari with me to our club on _____ or, "Kenya" come to our invitational tournament etc.

Decorations
Centerpieces of orchid plants that can be given away by raffle or a draw per table could be used.
Baskets of animal head covers make a fun centerpiece.
Allot one for each guest to be given as favors. African masks and baskets could also be used for centerpieces.

Favors
Animal jewelry
Animal print cosmetic bags or belts
Silk scarves with animal prints
Ostrich leather goods

Menu
Zambian groundnut soup
Tropical fruit cup
Tabbuli Salad
Wild Boar with yams
Chicken Tangine with olives and lemon
Sengalese cous cous
Dessert
Mango mousse

Format
1-2-3-3-2-1
Use 1 best ball on the 1st hole
Use 2 best balls on the 2nd hole
Use 3 best balls on the 3rd hole
Use 3 best balls on the 4th hole
Use 2 best balls on the 5th hole
Use 1 best ball on the 6th hole
Repeat for the remaining holes

Prizes
Wooden carved animals
Straw tote bags
Decoupaged ostrich eggs

Tiger's eye jewelry
Precious stone jewelry
Kruger and gold jewelry

Sources and information
www.kottlersafrica.com
Go to other specific web sites for African masks and baskets or food.

Mardi Gras Theme

Mardi Gras Theme

Mardi Gras has been a tradition since the Middle Ages. It is the last day before the religious fasting season of Lent. Mardi Gras is the French name for Shrove Tuesday. Literally translated, the term means "fat Tuesday." It was so called because it represented the last opportunity for merry-making and excessive indulgence in food and drink before the solemn season of fasting. The carnivals, with spectacular parades, masked balls, mock ceremonials and street dancing usually last for a week or more before Mardigras itself. Some of the most celebrated are held in New Orleans, Rio de Janeiro, Nice and Cologne.

Part of the Mardi Gras merrymaking is the eating of King Cakes, which are available at local bakeries–or online. King Cakes are decorated in the festive colors of purple, gold and green sugar icing. Each cake has a small plastic doll hidden inside and whoever finds the doll has to host the next party.

Invitations
Invitations can be brightly colored in the traditional colors of green, gold and purple, and depict, comedy/tragedy masks, feathered masks, king's crowns, etc.
Guests can be requested to come in costume or be masked.

Decorations
Streamers of purple, gold and green, wands, masks, beads, crowns. There are web sites where these decorations can be ordered. One is http://www.mardigrasoutlet.com. Table linens can also be done in the Mardi Gras colors. Pro-shop staff as greeters should also be wearing the colors, or crowns

Favors
CD's of New Orleans type jazz would make a nice favor.
Preservation Hall Jazz is a good example.

Menu
A favorite beverage in New Orleans is the Hurricane.
Naturally, Cajun type food is the order of the day.
If a continental breakfast is served, by all means use King Cakes. These can be created by your pastry chef. They are ring type coffee cakes decorated with icing in the Mardi Gras colors.
For lunch or dinner, do a shrimp Creole, gumbo, grits,

You could also have a shrimp boil, with peel and eat shrimp, grilled or blackened fish, hush puppies, and dirty rice. Other suggestions are Etouffes, Creole chicken, Red beans and Rice.
Bread pudding with whiskey sauce for dessert
Pralines, or pecan pies would also be appropriate.

Format
Mystery partners in nine hole matches, better ball.
Beads could be handed out for Mulligans.

Prizes
Weekend in New Orleans, Paul Prudhomme or Emeril cook books
Pro shop gift certificates.
Gift certificates to local restaurants.
Gift baskets with Cajun spices, sauces, pralines, coffee, beignets.

Mexican Theme

Mexican Theme

Invitations
Bright in color and can include, sombreros, serapes, guitars, chili peppers

Decorations
Centerpieces can be bouquets of Gerber Daisies, or vases of crepe paper flowers centered on a serape square. Sunflowers are also a good choice. Black and pinto beans can be spread on the table around the centerpiece. Another suggestion is a ring of chili peppers around a candle. Napkins should be bright colors, either different at each place setting, or the same color for each table, tied with raffia or bright ribbons. Maracas, sombreros, festival headdresses with ribbons and piñatas are good choices to add to the décor. Mexican decorations can be obtained over the internet.

Favors
Mexican silver or pottery.
Crate and Barrel carries tequila shot glass with a silver overlay that is handcrafted in Mexico and very attractive.
A molinillo, which is a Mexican whisk for mixing hot chocolate and the recipe for the chocolate at each place setting.
Check the web listing for sources.

Handmade windsock of brightly colored grosgrain ribbon for golf cart

Menu
Dishes of corn chips and salsa, Margaritas for beverages.
Gazpacho or tortilla soup
Salad of shredded lettuce, avocado, refried beans and sour cream.
Or
A mixed bean salad dressed with flavored oil and vinegar.
Main course.
Enchilada Chicken Casserole. Or a Taco Salad in large taco shell. Or make your own tacos, buffet style. Or chicken or beef fajitas with warm tortillas.
(See recipe index for Mexican recipes
Dessert
Fried ice cream or Mexican sopa pillas or flan
Alternate recipes are given as this tournament can work for all three classifications and for a one or two day tournament.

Either for luncheon, if a one day event, or for dinner if a two day event, hire a classical guitar player or a trio or small combo for music.

Format
Since this works well for all types of tournaments, for a mixed event use the usual gentleman host and guest lady as partners and the gentleman guest and host lady as partners. The first day use total of better ball of partners, and the second day have husbands and wives as partners with best ball of the foursome.
Do closest to the pin on the par threes.

Prizes
Talavera pottery or silver items.
Kamalico's glassware from Guadalhari

New Year's Eve Theme

New Year's Eve Theme

This is a good tournament for couples.

Invitations
Do artwork of streamers, confetti, champagne bottles, party hats noisemakers and clocks. Have the script read "Putting on the Glitz" and ask guests to dress glitzy.

Decorations
Centerpieces: top hats or ice buckets with cellophane and bottle of champagne
Black napkins on white tablecloth tied with gold and or silver ribbon. Sprinkle glitter around the centerpiece.

Favors
Give travel clocks or small table clocks or watches.

Menu
Fancy appetizers and cocktails,
The main course would be fillet of Beef Tenderloin served with béarnaise sauce.
Small roasted potatoes
Green beans
Caesars salad
For Dessert a chocolate or melba sauce parfait

Formats
Have the tournament in the afternoon and a party evening with a dinner dance.
Play the tournament Chapman style. *(See chapter on Formats)*

Prizes
Certificate for fitness spa
Energy bracelets
Leather bound daily calendars or date books.

Oktoberfest Theme

Oktoberfest Theme

Invitations
This would be a good mixed tournament. Design invitations with beer mugs, accordions, Lederhosen clad people, bratwurst. musical notes and autumn leaves.

Decorations
Tablecloths could be red and white checked. Use centerpieces of fall flowers. Have a bar set up with draft beer. Create a picnic style atmosphere. Play polka type music, or have a German Band. Ask the pro-shop staff to dress in white shirts, bow ties, suspenders, Tyrolean Hats.

Favors
Club logo designed beer steins
Carved nutcrackers or Christmas ornaments

Menu
Bratwurst and Knockwurst with buns
Hot German potato salad
Sauerkraut
Apple Strudel for dessert

Format
2 best balls of the foursome net and gross. Have husband and wives partners on the front nine and guests as partners of the hosts on the back nine.

Prizes
German Riesling wine
Wooden carved Christmas Ornaments
Cuckoo Clocks
Carved wooden nutcrackers
Music Boxes
Steins

Material Sources
www.oldworldnutcrackers.com
www.blackforrestfgifts.com/cuckoo.htm

Patriotic Theme

Patriotic Theme

Invitations
Ask guests to wear patriotic colors.
Flags, Banners, red white and blue.

Decorations
All manner of flags, buntings, Red White and Blue everywhere,
Tables, napkins, flowers,
Stars.

Favors
Patriotic watches
Tote Bags

Menu
Picnic fare, hamburgers, freedom fries, apple pie
Macaroni salad, brownies

Format
Flag tournament (note that the American flag should not be used in this format)

Prizes
Red, white, and blue dishes, coasters. glasses, tee shirts, visors, scarves, any article of clothing in the patriotic fabric. Other suggestions are, savings bonds. flags, umbrellas or jewelry.

Red Hat Theme

Red Hat Tournament

The Red Hat Society was developed as a result of a group of women deciding to greet middle age with verve, humor, and élan. They meet once a month for an outing usually for lunch. Participants are usually the age of 50+. They wear red hats and often purple articles of clothing as the uniform of their society. They are becoming evident all over the country. Underneath the frivolity, they share a bond of affection, forged by common life experiences and a genuine enthusiasm for wherever life takes them.

Develop this theme as follows:
Invitations can be a red hat on purple paper. Ask your guests to wear a red hat and something purple.

The following poem can be included in the invitation. Or posted at the club or used as a handout at luncheon perhaps read by the chairman.

Warning- When I am an Old Woman I Shall Wear Purple
By Jenny Joseph

When I am an old woman, I shall wear purple
With a red hat that doesn't go, and doesn't suit me.
And I shall spend my pension on brandy and summer gloves
And satin candles, and say we've no money for butter.
I shall sit down on the pavement when I am tired
And gobble up samples in shops and press alarm bells
And run my stick along the public railings
And make up for the sobriety of my youth.
I shall go out in my slippers in the rain
And pick the flowers in other people's gardens
And learn to spit.

You can wear terrible shirts and grow more fat
And eat three pounds of sausages at a go
Or only bread and pickles for a week
And hoard pens and pencils and beer nuts and things in boxes.

But now we must have clothes that keep us dry
And pay our rent and not swear in the street
And set a good example for the children.
We must have friends to dinner and read the papers.

But maybe I ought to practice a little now?
So people who know me are not too shocked and surprised
When suddenly I am old, and start to wear purple..

Decorations

Centerpieces can be hat forms with a red hat and purple tulle as draping. Tee decorations a red rose. Use red, purple or pink napkins.

Favors

A red or purple tote bag, or a red or purple fancy change purse.

Menu

Luncheon could be chicken crepes and a salad, with a divine chocolate dessert with red raspberry sauce.
(See recipe section for chocolate satin cake)
Serve a pinot noir for the wine.

Format

A fun one, not too serious. Perhaps, throwing out one of your worst holes on each nine. And don't forget mulligans.

Prizes

Whimsical—playing cards baskets of pink or purple bubble bath or other spa type items. Gift certificates for luncheon at local restaurants. Golf shirts of red, pink or purple. Red or purple tote bags, Red wine, Red scarves, Red, purple or pink lingerie, Red tee shirts, A bouquet of red or pink roses.

If a hole in one prize is offered—a red golf bag, red car or a garnet ring or bracelet.

Don't forget to request that your pro-shop staff wear red or purple shirts!!

Scottish Theme

Scottish Theme

Invitations
This one is easy, and can be applied to all ethnic type tournament themes. Just go with the culture. Invitations can make use of the Scotch Thistle or the kilt.

Decorations
First, plaids are the requirement of the day. Bag pipers are available and are a nice touch at the beginning and possibly at the end of the tournament. This theme would work for all three classifications of events i.e. men's, ladies', and mixed.

Table decorations could be squares of plaid fabric as center squares on the diagonal, with centerpieces of heather. Napkins in a strong solid color—red or green—tied with plaid ribbon for napkin rings. Pick up the colors of the plaid. Tams could also be used.

Menu
If breakfast is included Scottish scones with jam and clotted cream. Also possibly oat cakes or even oatmeal cookies would suffice.

For lunch or dinner, include Cock-a-leekie soup, or Scotch broth, salmon for the entrée—either cold poached on a bed of greens, or hot with creamed potatoes.
Dessert suggestion is cranachan with shortbread. *(See recipe index.)*
If there is a cocktail party of course cold smoked salmon with lime and capers is a must.

Format
Any of the best ball tournaments work well in most any tournament. Mulligans– with advice to "save them and use them prudently" on the score cards. Stickers depicting a thistle would be great for these.

Prizes
Scottish Crystal or pottery which usually includes the thistle emblem. Also for a mixed or men's tournament a bottle of good scotch whiskey. There are also crystal glasses made by Ridel specifically for single malt scotch. Check the internet for these.

Signs of the Zodiac
Theme

Signs of the Zodiac Theme

Invitations
Picture stars, moons or actual zodiac signs.
Invite guests to fly to the moon and play among the stars.

Decorations
Again astrological signs, stars, moons, crystal balls.
You could use Jade plants for centerpieces.
Napkins in sky blue wrapped with star garland.
Chinese restaurants have paper placements depicting the animal astrological signs and are fun and entertaining.

Favors
Crystal prisms
Jade jewelry
Dream catchers

Menu
Most people involved in the Zodiac or Astrology are vegetarians. So a wonderfully composed salad or a stir fry would be good choices for the entrée. The chicken nectarine salad in the recipe chapter might work. Or the tomato onion pie, served with crescent rolls. A fruit dessert with cookies cut into stars or moons would be in keeping with the theme.

Format
5 and 4
Total of 1st five holes on the front 9 and last 4 holes on back 9
Subtract 1/2 handicap

Prizes
In Chinese culture, jade symbolizes nobility, perfection, constancy and immortality. Ornaments of jade, either figures, or jewelry would be a fine choice for prizes of this theme. A good website to browse is http://www.joyluckship.com

Other prize suggestions are:
Books on the Zodiac
Stained glass star catchers
Dream Catchers
Compact Discs of Cosmic type music
Aromatherapy bath oils
Candles

Wind Chimes
Crystals (cosmic creations.com)
Certificates for Massage therapy

St. Patrick's Day Theme

St. Patrick's Day Tournament Theme

Invitations
Invitations can be quarter-fold or half-fold or flyer type.
Use St. Patrick's Day clip art. Designs usually include hats, leprechauns, clay pipes, shamrocks, pots of gold.
Invite your guests to wear green.

Decorations
Decorations would follow the invitation theme. Use white tablecloths with green napkins. For centerpieces a shamrock plant sitting on a green square, with plastic shamrocks strewn about. You could also use a bouquet of green carnations.

Favors could be little bags of gold wrapped chocolate coins. Or more elaborately Waterford or like crystal bud vases or ring holders would make nice favors.

Menu
Potato soup
Irish Stew or corned beef and cabbage
Soda Bread
Lime sorbet topped with crème de menthe and shamrock shaped cookies.
Grasshopper pie *(See recipe mix)* could also be served.

Format
Better ball of partners
Net and Gross
A special prize could be given for a birdie on a particular hole, and call it the "pot of gold"
Mulligans could be issued as shamrock or Leprechaun stickers

Ask your pro-shop staff to wear green shirts.

Prizes
Irish Crystal
Beleek china pieces
Irish knitted (fisherman style) afghans, sweaters, scarves.
A bottle of Irish Crème Irish Whiskey

Thanksgiving Theme

Thanksgiving Theme

Invitations
Turkeys, cornucopia, fall flowers

Decorations
Centerpiece: cornucopia with fruit and vegetables or
a floral centerpiece. Use autumn colors of gold, brown, orange and
red for linens. Autumn leaves could be strewn on the table if they
are available. Soak them in mineral oil overnight and dry with paper
towels to avoid curling.

Favors
Large decorative serving spoon

Menu
If the tournament is played in the a.m. with luncheon, serve a
turkey casserole (turkey cranberry casserole, turkey tetrazzini or
turkey crepes. *(See recipe index)*
A molded cranberry salad
Corn Bread Sticks
Pumpkin pie or pumpkin strudel *(See recipe index)*
If the tournament includes a dinner, have a traditional turkey din-
ner menu.

Format
Shoot out scramble

Prizes
Award fresh turkeys for long drive, closest to the line and closest to
the pins.
Other prizes could be turkey platters, paper goods, or certificates
for a floral arrangement.

Valentine's Day Theme

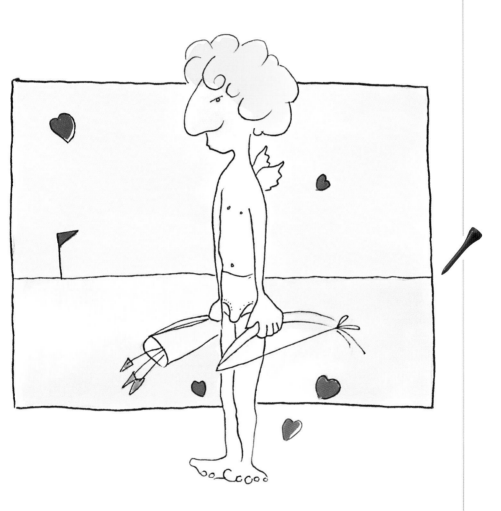

Valentine's Day Theme

Invitations
Appropriate for theme, flowers, hearts, cupids

Decorations
Red or pink napkins tied with lace. Centerpieces of red tulips or carnations.

Favors
Small boxes of chocolates tied with red and white ribbon. Many candy manufacturers have special boxes for the day.

Menu
Tomato Basil Soup
Cranberry chicken (see the recipe index) with rice
Baby beet salad with greens. Cherry muffins.
Strawberry cheesecake for dessert

Format
Scramble for nine holes and two best balls of the foursome for nine holes. The pro-shop has a formula for handicapping.

Prizes
Dishes in the shape of hearts
Red dishes or cookware.
Lacy lingerie
Travel cosmetic bags or jewelry cases.
Paper goods with the heart motif.

Victorian Tea Theme

Victorian Tea Theme

If you close your eyes and think Victorian-what comes to mind?? Pastel colors, lace, feathers, everything feminine. This is definitely a ladies event.

Invitation
Use delicate, flowery invitations.

Ask the pro-shop staff to wear dark pants, white shirts and bow ties.

Decorations
Use centerpieces of all different teapots filled with flowers. Table cloths should be white with a lace overlay or a square of lace in the center. Give the teapots away for special birthdays or anniversaries closest to the date of the tournament. Alternatively, use flowers for centerpieces and the teapots could be prizes. Napkins in pastel colors, either the same for each table or mixed. Use paper lace dollies on soup or dessert saucers.

Favors
Umbrellas.
Lavender sachet pillows.
Magnification glasses on chains.

Menu
Continental breakfast to include special pastries, juice, coffee and tea. Treats at half way points, cups of cut up fruit and a cookie.

Luncheon menu: Vichyssoise, a special chicken soufflé and fresh vegetables. A molded salad, perhaps, tomato aspic. Have a wonderful dessert. Try the chocolate truffle tart with crème anglaise and caramel sauce. *(see recipe index)*

Plan to take pictures and have them positioned at each table place setting. If you can find it, or have someone paint a board with Victorian garbed ladies with a place for the participant's heads, it would be novel. For a small donation, village theater groups often have costumes that you could borrow to costume the hostess.

Nosegay bouquets could be used as tee markers. *(Directions will follow)*

Format

Nine holes 1 best ball of the foursome, nine holes 2 best balls of the foursome. 90% handicap.

Prizes

All things feminine. Lacy pillows, picture frames, shawls, throws, elegant bud vases. Cache pots with violet plants. Fancy bathroom hand towels. Gift certificates from the local florist, spa, or dress shop. Perfume atomizers, candles, lacy placemats, bedside water carafe with glass, wicker bed tray, and breakfast china set.

Nosegay bouquets

Nosegay bouquets can be made from any flowers. Cut the stems all the same length, about 10" long, or to fit a particular vase. Gather the flowers one by one in your hand into a tight bundle. Surround the flowers with some green leaves. Tie tightly with raffia. This bouquet can then be inserted into a paper lace doily or you can use fabric. Place in water and they will last for several days. Nosegays can be used for Tee markers or in a group as centerpieces or as individual place settings.

Western Theme

Western Theme

Suitable for all types of tournaments

Invitations or flyers
Cowboys, neckerchiefs, horses, wagons.
Ask guests to try and dress appropriately, especially for the dinner night. Blue jeans are acceptable.
Pro-shop staff to be attired in cowboy hats, and kerchiefs, bright shirts and blue jeans.

Decorations
Use bales of hay, bright colored bandannas, cowboy hats, lasoos, spurs.
Dinner night if inside, could depict a western saloon, with waitresses and waiters dressed accordingly. A swinging saloon door could be fashioned at the entrance.
Tables could be covered with poker chips and playing cards. Have a centerpiece of cowboy hats and or boots. Cactus plants would also work.

Menu
If the event can be held outside a chuck wagon is used as the buffet table. (This could also be incorporated if the buffet is to be inside.) Use a large bushel basket of daisies at the top and feature barbeque, with pulled pork and several sauces and fried chicken and ribs. Thick sliced bread, cole slaw, corn on the cob, sliced tomatoes and baked beans. A variety of desserts including cobbler, or make your own sundaes. Of course bar service is also required. Offer snacks of popcorn and pretzels.

Country music is the order of the night. Square dances can be a lot of fun. Hire a caller.

Favors
A special barbeque tool like a special temperature sensing fork or a "Barbie", or a "Pigtail".

Format
If it is a two day mixed tournament first nine holes best ball of lady guest and host and best ball of male guest and hostess. Second nine holes scramble. Second day two best balls of the foursome added to the previous day score. Full handicap with a maximum of 36.

If it is a one day tournament one best ball of the foursome net and gross. Or one best ball of partners.

If a men's or ladies' two day tournament have a ringer tournament.

Prizes
A set of barbeque tools or some type of barbeque grill. Like a George Forman Grill or Hibachi Grill.
Basket of barbeque supplies
Wood chips, as hickory or maple
Barbeque Sauces
Barbeque cook book
Gift certificate for pair of cowboy boots

Recipe Suggestions

Recipes

The recipe suggestions in the book are just that—suggestions. Certainly the chefs have their own ideas and methods. The menus are only a starting point for planning purposes. Most chefs are more than open to suggestion and can generally improve upon them.

The recipes are indexed and they have all been taste tested. The sources will be listed at the bottom of the recipe.

Recipe Index

Swedish

Lighter Entrees

Regular Entrees

Berry Cookie Cobbler

2 bags (12 oz.) ea. frozen mixed berries, thawed
1 container (21 oz.) apple pie filling
⅓ c. granulated sugar
1-½ teaspoons ground cinnamon
1 roll (18 oz.) prepared sugar cookie dough.
Vanilla ice cream.

Preheat oven to 350 degrees
In a large bowl, mix berries, apple pie filling, sugar, and cinnamon.
Transfer fruit mixture to an 8x8x2 inch baking dish.
Crumble cookie dough over fruit, covering thickly and completely.
Bake uncovered until cookie crust is golden and crisp, and juices
bubble thickly about 45 minutes.
Serve warm with ice cream.

These cobblers can also be made in individual ramekins.

Recipe Source: *Semi-Homemade Cooking by Sandra Lee*

Zucchini Bread

3 eggs
1 c. oil
2 c. sugar
2 tsp. vanilla
1-½ tsp. cinnamon
1 tsp. salt
1 can (8-¼ oz) crushed pineapple well-drained
1 c. each copped dates and pecans

2 tsp. baking soda
3 c. flour
2 c. shredded zucchini
¾ tsp. nutmeg
¼ tsp. baking powder

Beat eggs, oil, sugar, and vanilla until thick. Stir in remaining ingredients. Mix well. Pour into 2 well greased 9"x5" loaf pans. Bake at
350 degrees for 1 hour.

Recipe Source: *Dot Thomson*

Chocolate Satin Cake or Tasmanian Devils Food Cake

1 - 8oz. pkg. cream cheese
1 ½ c. sugar divided
½ c. water
5 large eggs
12 oz. semisweet chocolate chips
½ lb. butter

Preheat oven to 375 degrees with rack in the center of the oven. Butter a 9" cake pan and place a circle of parchment in the bottom of the pan. Butter the paper also. Combine cream cheese and ½ c. sugar. Mix well with electric mixer for 4 minutes. Add eggs one at a time and mix until incorporated. Place remaining sugar and water in a saucepan and bring to a boil. Add chocolate, remove from heat and mix until melted. Add butter a little at a time. Mix well until fully incorporated. Add chocolate mixture to cream cheese mixture. Mix until smooth. Pour batter into prepared pan. Bake in a water bath for approximately one hour or until firm. Cool completely. Loosen from sides of pan with a knife. Remove from pan and remove circle of parchment paper.

Spread with the following glaze:
4 oz. heavy cream, scalded
6 oz. semisweet chocolate chips.
Heat cream to a boil. Remove from heat. Add chocolate. Mix. Stir over ice water until smooth and slightly thickened. Pour over cake, spreading evenly.
Cut with a sharp knife. Serve with whipped cream and raspberries.

Serves 16

Source: *Cathy Kirk*

Chocolate Truffle Tart

Heat oven to 300

1 cup pecans, toasted & coarsely ground
1 cup graham cracker crumbs
4 tbsp. Butter melted
2 tbsp. Sugar
Combine the above and press into the bottom and 1 ½" up the sides of a 9" springform pan.

In a saucepan heat 1 pound semisweet chocolate, chopped, in 1 cup heavy cream until chocolate is melted. Transfer to bowl and set aside. In a separate large bowl, combine 6 beaten eggs, and ⅔ cup sugar and beat until thick and pale in color. Fold in ⅓ cup flour and mix well. Fold in melted chocolate. Pour into prepared springform pan. Bake in oven for 45 minutes. Cool. Serve with Crème Anglaise and Caramel Sauce. Dust with powdered sugar.

Crème Anglaise:
In a small bowl, whisk together 3 egg yolks and ¼ cup sugar until pale in color. Set aside. In saucepan bring 1 cup heavy cream and ¼ teasp. vanilla to a boil, stirring constantly. Remove from heat. Pour one-fourth of the hot cream mixture into the egg yolk mixture. Mix well. Transfer the entire yolk mixture into the saucepan containing the hot cream mixture. Cook over medium heat until sauce thickens and coats the back of a wooden spoon. Remove from heat. Strain into clean bowl, stir until cool.

Caramel Sauce:
2 cups sugar
½ cup butter
1 cup whipping cream
1 tsp. Vanilla

Heat a heavy skillet over medium heat until heat penetrates through the bottom of the pan. Add sugar. Stir with a wooden spoon until sugar melts to a golden syrup. (Do not overcook as this will scorch easily.) Remove from heat and add butter. When butter has melted, add cream a little at a time, stirring constantly. Stir in vanilla. Cool. Store in a covered glass container and refrigerate. Keeps for several weeks.

Nap plates with caramel, add a small slice of tart and decorate with Crème Anglaise and powdered sugar. Berries may be added for color.
Source: *The Common Grill Cookbook*

Grasshopper Ice Cream Pie

1 c. chocolate wafer crumbs
2 tbsp. butter, melted
2 tbsp. 1% low –fat milk
1-7 oz. jar marshmallow crème
¼ c. green crème de menthe
2 tbsp. white crème de cocoa
1-8 oz. container frozen fat-free whipped topping, thawed
3 c. vanilla low-fat ice cream softened
2 tsp. chocolate syrup

Combine crumbs and butter in a small bowl, stir with a fork until moist. Press into bottom of a 9 inch springform pan. Chill. Combine milk and marshmallow crème in a microwave-safe bowl; microwave at HIGH 1 minute, stirring once. Add crème de menthe, crème de cacao, and whipped topping, stirring until blended. Spread ice cream into prepared pan; top with marshmallow mixture. Freeze at least 6 hours. Drizzle with chocolate syrup before serving.

Yield: 12 servings.

Source: *Southern Living Magazine*

Pot de Crème

Yield six small servings

2 eggs
1 cup semi sweet chocolate chips
4 tablespoons sugar
¾ cup whole milk scalded
1 teaspoon Vanilla

Blend all at low for 1 minute. Pour into individual cups and chill. Serve with whipped cream.

Do Not Double.

Source: *Nat Whiting*

Pumpkin Strudel

1 - 15oz. can pumpkin
½ c. packed brown sugar
½ tsp. ground cinnamon
½ tsp. ground ginger
½ tsp. nutmeg
½ tsp. salt
12 sheets frozen fillo dough
⅔ c. butter, melted
1 c. granulated sugar
4 tsp. ground cinnamon
1 c. chopped pecans
1 - 8 oz. pkg. cream cheese, cut into 12 slices
Whipped Cream

Preheat oven to 400 degrees. For filling, in a small bowl combine pumpkin, brown sugar, spices, and salt. Set aside. Place 2 sheets of fillo on top of one another, brush top sheet with some of the better. (Keep remaining fillo covered with plastic wrap or a damp towel to prevent it from becoming dry and brittle.) In a small bowl combine granulated sugar and 4 tsp. cinnamon. Sprinkle a generous 2 tbsp. of sugar cinnamon mixture over the brushed fillo. Sprinkle with about 2 tbsp. of the pecans. Cut the 2 layered sheets of phyllo lengthwise to create two long strips. Place a slice of cream cheese about 2 inches from end of dough strip. Spoon a well rounded tablespoon of pumpkin mixture on top of the cream cheese. To shape, fold bottom edge of fillo up and over the filling. Fold insides and roll up to encase the filling. Place on a baking sheet, seam side down. Brush with some of the melted butter. Repeat with remaining ingredients. Sprinkle with any remaining sugar cinnamon mixture. Bake for15 minutes or until lightly browned.

Yield: 12 servings.

Source: *Better Homes & Gardens Magazine*

Outback Steakhouse Coconut Shrimp

1 ½ lb. large raw shrimp
½ c. flour
½ c. cornstarch
1 t. salt
½ t. white pepper
2 tbsp. vegetable oil
1 c. ice water
Oil for deep frying
2 c. short shredded coconut
½ c. orange marmalade
½ c Grey Poupon country mustard
½ c. honey
3-4 drops Tabasco sauce

Peel devein and wash shrimp. Dry well on paper towels. Set aside. In a bowl, mix all dry ingredients for batter. Add 2 tbsp. oil and ice water. Stir to blend. To fry: heat oil to 350 degrees in deep fryer or electric skillet. Spread coconut on a flat pan a little at a time, adding more as needed. Dip shrimp in batter, then roll in coconut. Fry in hot oil until lightly browned. About 4 minutes. Bake at 300 degrees, 5 minutes to finish cooking.

Serve with sweet and sour sauce of the following:
Combine marmalade, mustard, honey and Tabasco sauce to taste.

Source: *The Internet*

Turkey Tetrazzini

Topping
½ c. fresh breadcrumbs
a pinch of salt
1 ½ tablespoons unsalted butter, melted
1 oz. Parmesan cheese, grated

Filling:
6 tbsp. (¾ stick) unsalted butter, plus extra for baking dish
8 oz. white mushrooms, cleaned and sliced thin
2 medium onions, chopped fine
Salt and fresh ground pepper
¾# spaghetti or other long strand pasta strands snapped in half
½ c. flour
2 c. chicken stock or canned low sodium chicken broth
3 tbsp. dry sherry
3 oz. Parmesan cheese, grated
½ tsp. grated nutmeg
2 tsp. juice from 1 small lemon
2 tsp. minced fresh thyme leaves
2 c. frozen peas
4 c. leftover cooked boneless turkey or chicken cut into 1" inch pieces

For the topping:
Adjust oven rack to middle position and heat oven to 350 degrees. Mix breadcrumbs, salt, and butter in small baking dish; bake until golden brown and crisp, 15 to 20 minutes. Cool to room temperature and mix with ¼ c. grated Parmesan cheese in a small bowl. Set aside.

For the filling:
Increase oven temperature to 450 degrees. Heat 2 Tbsp. butter in a large skillet over medium heat until foaming subsides; add mushrooms and onions and sauté, stirring frequently, until onions soften and mushroom liquid evaporates, 12 to 15 minutes. Season with salt and ground black pepper to taste; transfer to medium bowl and set aside. Meanwhile, cook pasta in large pot of boiling, salted water until al dente. Reserve ¼ cup cooking water, drain spaghetti, and return to pot with reserved liquid.

For the sauce:
Melt remaining 4 Tbsp. butter in a clean skillet over medium heat. When foam subsides, whisk in flour and cook, whisking constantly, until flour turns golden, 1 to 2 minutes. Whisking constantly, gradually add chicken stock. Adjust heat to medium-high and simmer until mixture thickens, 3 to 4 minutes. Off heat, whisk in sherry, Parmesan, nutmeg, ½ tsp. salt, lemon juice, and thyme. Add sauce, sautéed vegetables, peas, and meat to spaghetti and mix well; adjust seasonings to taste. Turn mixture into a buttered 13 x 9 inch baking dish, sprinkle with reserved breadcrumbs, and bake until breadcrumbs brown and mixture is bubbly, 13 to 15 minutes. Serve immediately.

Yield eight servings.

Source: *Fine Cooking Magazine*

Enchilada Casserole

1 medium onion, chopped
2 tbsp. vegetable oil
1 - 19oz.can enchilada sauce
1 - 16oz.can black beans drained and rinsed
1 - 14oz. can diced tomatoes with jalapenos
1 - 11 oz can Mexican-style corn, drained
1 tsp. chili powder
1 tsp. ground cumin
1 - 10oz, package 6 inch corn tortillas
3 c. chopped cooked chicken (or 2# lean ground beef, cooked)
3 cups shredded Mexican four cheese blend

Sauté onion in hot oil over medium high heat until tender. Stir in next 6 ingredients. Reduce heat to low and cook, stirring often, 5 minutes or until thoroughly heated. Spoon one third of sauce mixture into a lightly greased 13x9 inch baking dish. Layer with one third of tortillas, half of the chopped chicken, and 1 cup cheese. Repeat layers with one third each of sauce mixture and tortillas, remaining chicken and 1 cup cheese. Top with remaining tortillas, sauce mixture and 1 cup cheese. Bake at 350 degrees for 15-20 minutes or until golden and bubbly.

Source: *Mexican Cooking by Owlswood Productions*

Botana Dip

2 cans frito lay bean dip
3 avacados
2 tbsp. lemon juice
¼ tsp. salt
¼ tsp. pepper.

Mix together.
½ c. mayo. 8 oz sour cream, 1 pkg. taco seasoning mix.

Mix together.
Two chopped tomatoes
One can pitted black olives chopped
8 oz cheddar cheese shredded

Place each item in a dish in layers in the order listed above and serve with plain traditional taco chips.

Source: *Pat Arney*

Coffee Caramel Orange Custard

⅓ c. sugar
6 eggs
2 tbsp. coffee liqueur
3 tbsp. honey
1 ¾ c. milk
½ tsp. grated orange rind

Melt the sugar in a 9 inch pie pan over moderately high heat, holding pan with potholders and tipping and tilting it so sugar caramelizes evenly and coats sides and bottom of the pan. Set aside to cool and harden. Beat together eggs, coffee liqueur and honey, then gradually mix in milk and orange rind. Pour into caramel-lined pan and place in a larger pan in a water bath. Bake at 325 degrees for 35 to 40 minutes, until a knife inserted near center comes out clean. Chill. Loosen edge, and then invert custard carefully onto a rimmed serving dish. Cut into wedges, spooning the caramel sauce over each serving.
Yield 6 servings.

Source: *Mexican Cooking*
Owlswood Productions

Cock-A-Leekie Soup

1 plump chicken
⅔ Bunches of leeks
1 doz.prunes (optional)
2qts. Beef or Veal stock
Salt and pepper to taste

Truss the fowl and place in a large pot with the stock and three or four leeks, blanched and chopped. Bring to the boil and cook gently for two hours or until the fowl is tender, and remove from stock. Skim off the fat with paper. Add the leeks, and salt and pepper to taste. Simmer very gently until the leeks are tender. Half an hour before serving, the prunes may be added whole. Some minced chicken can be added. Not in the tradition, but some cooks add two tablespoonfuls of rice.

Source: *Recipes from Scotland*
F. Marian McNeill

Cranachan or Cream-Crowdie

Heavy cream
Oatmeal
Fine Sugar
Rum or Vanilla flavoring
Fresh berries

Toast some oatmeal lightly in a frying pan or in the oven. This gives it an agreeable, somewhat nutty flavor. Beat a bowlful of cream to a stiff froth, and stir in a handful or two of oatmeal, with the cream predominating. Sweeten to taste and add flavoring. Add fresh berries and serve in a crystal dish.

Scots Shortbread

8 oz. flour
4 oz. rice flour
8 oz. butter
4 oz. fine sugar

Put the butter and sugar on a board and work with the hand until thoroughly incorporated. Mix the two flours, and gradually work into the butter and sugar until the dough resembles short crust. Do not roll out, but press with the hands into two round cakes, either in oiled and floured wooden shortbread moulds, or on a sheet of parchment paper. The best thickness is one inch for a cake eight inches in diameter. Pinch the edges neatly with finger and thumb, and prick all over with a fork. Bake in 300 degree oven until lightly browned. 45 to 50 minutes. Remove to a rack and let cool until barely warm. Cut almost through the dough and if desired sprinkle with sugar. Let stand until completely cool and gently retrace the cuts and separate the pieces.

Source: *The Internet*

Lemon Curd

Grate rind of one lemon.
Juice of one lemon
3 whole eggs
½ c. butter
1 c. white sugar

Cook over double boiler stirring constantly until thick. Refrigerate in a jar. Used for tart fillings, cake filling.

Source: *Gladys Cain*

Caramel Sauce

2 c. sugar
½ c. butter
1 c. whipping cream
1 tsp. vanilla

Heat a heavy cast iron pan over medium heat until heat penetrates through the bottom of the pan. Add sugar, stir with wooden spoon until sugar melts to a golden colored syrup. (Do not overcook this scorches easily.) Remove from heat, add butter. When butter is melted, add cream a little at a time, stirring constantly. Stir in vanilla. Store in a covered glass container and refrigerate. Will keep for several weeks.

Source: *Cathy Kirk*

Melting Moments

½ c. cornstarch
½ c. powdered sugar
¾ c. butter
1 c. sifted flour
granulated sugar for rolling

Stir together cornstarch, sugar and flour. Stir in shortening to form a soft dough. Chill 1 hour. Form in one inch balls and roll in granulated sugar. Stamp with cookie stamp on an ungreased cookie sheet, or flatten with a glass. Bake at 350 degrees for 20-25 minutes.

Yield 2 ½ doz.

Source: *Cathy Kirk*

White Oven Scones

1 lb. flour
1 tsp. Baking soda
2 tsp. cream of Tartar
$\frac{1}{2}$ tsp. salt
1 oz. sugar
3 oz. butter
1 egg
Milk to moisten.

Sift the flour, soda and cream of tartar into a bowl, add the salt and sugar: rub in the butter. Beat the egg and pour into a well in the flour mixture, with enough milk to make a very soft dough. Turn on to a floured board, sprinkle with flour, roll out or pat out to a half-inch thickness, cut into rounds or triangles, and bake in a 425 degree oven 12-15 minutes.

Source: *The Internet*

Swedish Pancakes

7 - 8 eggs
3 - 3-$\frac{1}{2}$ c. whole milk
1/4 c. sugar
2 tsp. salt
1-$\frac{1}{2}$ c -2 c. flour

Beat all together, batter will be thin. Place small amt. of batter in buttered pan and rotate pan to spread batter.   Flip when brown. Serves 6-8 people.
Serve with lingon berries.

Source: *Mary Bengtsson*

Cheese, Onion, Tomato Quiche

Crust
10" pastry crust or frozen 9" deep dish pie crust and put into 10" pan. Chill crust.

5 oz. gruyere cheese
2 large tomatoes
5 oz. Swiss cheese
2 eggs
2 tbsp. flour
¾ c. cream
4 tbsp. butter
nutmeg
2 large onions
1 t. Basil
5 oz. gruyere cheese

Grate Swiss and gruyere cheeses and toss with flour. Melt butter. Slice onions into the butter and sauté gently until golden. Spread ½ cheese mixture over crust. Spread onions over cheese. Sauté slices of tomatoes in butter left from onions. Sprinkle tomatoes with basil. Arrange tomatoes over onions and cover remaining cheese mixture. Beat eggs with cream and pour over cheese. Sprinkle top with nutmeg. Bake at 350 degrees for 35-40 min. Can be made day before and reheated before serving.

Serves 6 as main dish.

Source: *Carol Schuetz*

Florentine Crepe Cups

3 eggs slightly beaten
⅔ c. flour
½ tsp. salt
1 cup milk

1 ½ c. shredded cheddar cheese
3 tbsp. flour
3 eggs slightly beaten
⅔ c. sour cream
10 oz. pkg. frozen chopped spinach, thawed, drained and squeezed dry
4 oz. can mushrooms drained, or 8-10 fresh sautéed with shallots
6 crispy cooked bacon slices, crumbled
½ tsp. salt
Dash of pepper

Combine eggs, flour, salt and milk: beat until smooth. Let stand 30 minutes. For twelve crepes, pour 2 tbsp. batter into hot lightly greased 8 inch skillet. Cook on one side only, underside is lightly browned. Toss cheese with flour, add remaining ingredients: mix well. Fit crepes into greased muffin pan: fill with cheese mixture. Bake at 350 degrees for 40 minutes or until set. Garnish with bacon curls, if desired.

Source: *Janet Nikoden*

Grilled Chicken and Nectarine Salad

4 skinless boneless chicken breast halves
4 tbsp. fresh lime juice
2 tbsp. fresh chopped thyme or 2 tsp. dried
1 tsp. plus 1 tbsp. olive oil

1 small clove garlic, minced
5 med. Nectarines, thinly sliced
6 c. packed torn mixed salad greens

1 tbsp. pine nuts, toasted
½ c. fresh raspberries

Place chicken in a shallow dish. Sprinkle with 1 tbsp. lime juice, 1 tablespoon thyme and 1 tsp. oil. Season with salt and pepper. Turn to coat. Cover and refrigerate from 1-4 hours.

Preheat barbecue grill to Med.- High heat or heat large nonstick skillet over Med. High heat. Grill or sauté chicken until golden brown, and just cooked through, about 5 minutes per side. Cool. Cut chicken across grain in thin diagonal slices.

Whisk 3 tbsp. lime juice, 1 tbsp. thyme, 1 tbsp. oil and garlic in a large bowl. Season with salt and pepper. Place nectarine slices in a small bowl; add 1 tbsp. dressing and toss to coat. Add salad greens to remaining dressing; toss to coat. Divide salad greens equally among 4 plates. Arrange sliced chicken atop each. Top with nectarines. Sprinkle with pine nuts. Garnish with raspberries.

Source: *Bon Appetite Magazine*

Hot Chicken Salad Casserole

Serves 5-6
Doubles or triples well

2 cups cooked chicken tenders cut in chunks
1 can Cream of Chicken soup, undiluted
¾ cup mayonnaise
1 cup diced celery
1 cup cooked rice
¼ cup grated onion
1 tbsp. Lemon juice
½ tsp. Salt
Pepper
1 small can sliced water chestnuts

Topping:
1 cup crushed cornflakes, buttered
½ cup slivered almonds

Bake in buttered casserole at 375 degrees for 20-30 minutes. You can also add 1 can chopped artichokes

Source: *Peg Nikoden*

Apricot-Chicken Roll-ups

1 - 6-7 oz pkg. dried apricots, snipped (about 1 ⅓ cups)
½ c. dried cranberries
3 tbsp. honey
1-½ t. ground or fresh ginger
⅔ c. fine dry bread crumbs
2 tbsp. snipped fresh parsley
1 tbsp. flour
1 tbsp. finely shredded parmesan cheese
1 tsp. paprika
½ tsp. sugar
½ tsp. salt
½ tsp. garlic powder
¼ tsp. onion powder
½ tsp. each oregano and thyme
2 tbsp. shortening
2 eggs
6 med. Skinless, boneless, chicken breast halves.

Preheat oven to 350 degrees. Coat a 3 qt. rectangular baking dish with nonstick cooking spray, set aside. Stir together apricots, cranberries, honey and ginger: set aside. Stir together dry ingred. Cut in shortening until mixture resembles fine crumbs. Transfer to a shallow dish. Place eggs in another shallow dish, beat lightly with a fork. With a meat mallet lightly pound each chicken breast between two pieces of plastic wrap into a rectangle slightly less than ¼" thick. Remove wrap. Spoon a scant ¼ c. of apricot mixture onto center of each chicken breast. Fold in bottom and sides. Roll up. Secure with toothpicks if necessary. Dip in egg, then in crumb mixture. Place in prepared dish. Bake 30-40".

Source: *Better Homes & Gardens Magazine*

Cranberry Chicken

1 can whole berry cranberry sauce
1 bottle Catalina salad dressing
1 package Lipton's onion soup mix

Combine above ingredients and pour evenly over 6 split boneless, skinless chicken breasts. Cover and refrigerate overnight if desired. Bake uncovered at 350 degrees for one hour.

Source: *Jeanne Lambdin*

Chicken with Rice

1 box Uncle Ben's Wild Rice Original
1 can cream of mushroom soup
1 can cream of chicken soup
1 can cream of celery soup
½ c. milk, ½ c. melted butter, ½ c. sherry
6 boneless skinless chicken breasts cut in half.
1 pkg. slivered almonds
2 oz. parmesan cheese

Butter a 9 x 13 pan

Spread rice and seasonings in pan. Mix soups, milk, butter and sherry. Pour ½ of mixture over rice. Add chicken and remaining sauce. Sprinkle with almonds and parmesan cheese. Bake 2-2-½ hours at 250 degrees. Can prepare night before and refrigerate and cook the following day.

Source: *Bev Howland*

Ordering Information:

Additional copies may be obtained through:
www.mjnpublishing/teeparties.com

By Phone:
828-898-5868

Or by mail:
Tee Parties
PO Box 1782
Banner Elk, NC 28604

Please send me _____ copies of "Tee Parties" at $24.95 + $5.00 shipping and handling. If sold in NC there will be an additional 7% tax of ($1.75).

Payment may be made by check, money order or Visa.
Please make checks payable to "Tee Parties"